# SHADOWS COME AT MIDNIGHT

*From PTSD to Purpose*

 **FriesenPress**

Suite 300 - 990 Fort St
Victoria, BC, V8V 3K2
Canada

www.friesenpress.com

Copyright © 2021 by Ross A. MacInnes
First Edition — 2021

All rights reserved.

No part of this publication may be reproduced in any form, or by any means, electronic or mechanical, including photocopying, recording, or any information browsing, storage, or retrieval system, without permission in writing from FriesenPress.

ISBN
978-1-5255-9467-0 (Hardcover)
978-1-5255-9466-3 (Paperback)
978-1-5255-9468-7 (eBook)

1. BIOGRAPHY & AUTOBIOGRAPHY, LAW ENFORCEMENT

Distributed to the trade by The Ingram Book Company

## DEDICATED TO

My wife, Dee, the most fantastic spouse, and helpmate in the world. The one who walked beside me through those dark and troubled times. I love you.

My children, Heather and Jordie, whose dad was absent from so many holiday celebrations, school events, or sporting occasions as he was on-shift, on-assignment, or on-call. I am proud to be your dad.

I am so blessed to have the family I do.

To the families of first responders, military vets, and front-line workers—you are the anchors that keep us from being dashed on the rocks from the constant storms. We can never thank you enough. You continue to support us and love us (even when we aren't that lovable sometimes).

And to the vets and those still serving: IGY6

Ross MacInnes

# CHAPTER ONE

*Get your ass out of bed, grab your shit, and get down to the garage!*

I had just drifted off to sleep when I was grabbed by the foot, shaken violently, and ordered back into uniform and down to the police cars. What in the hell had happened?

I was fresh out of RCMP training in Regina and partnered with Constable Donald Pearson doing general police duties west of Edmonton, Alberta. We were operating two separate patrol cars to cover the sprawling detachment area more effectively. I patrolled south toward the small town of Devon and a local ski center named Rabbit Hill. Donny took the calls at Winterburn and Spruce Grove, small towns that lay closer to the city limits.

We met up and decided to call it a night and head back to the Post Garage to put the cars away. But Donny took another call—alone. There had been a drunken fight at an all-night cafe, but it was over when Donny got there. As Donny was leaving, one of the participants came back, walked in with a rifle, and shot Donny. That was my introduction to life as a cop.

★ ★ ★

I was just a kid from back-ass Manitoba. The whole house was smaller than the average single-car garage. One-bedroom. One closet. The kitchen served as a dining room, living room, rec room, and porch. Six of us lived there—Mom, Dad, my three brothers, and me.

Dad set the standard of behavior—not just in the home, but in our overall actions in life. He had survived the Great Depression, had a profound (fervent, some would say) faith in God, and raised his family with frugality and religious belief and practice. Church three times on Sunday and twice in the middle of the week. We were Plymouth Brethren—of the old style. Women and girls' heads were required covering with hats or scarves; men the only ones allowed to pray out loud, preach, or lead the singing. And communion is held every Sunday. No work on the Lord's Day, billiards outlawed, and other denominations suspect (except Baptists—they were probably OK).

A highlight of our year (at least for the adults) was the annual conference in Winnipeg. Held on Thanksgiving weekend, the gathering covered three full days. Missionaries from Africa or South America would come and share their stories of lives changed, and souls saved. Shantymen, who were "itinerant preachers" living in lumber camps, would preach a couple of sermons, and lunch was always communal and well provided.

The second day, my brothers and I were tossing around a football when I spotted a young lady seated under a tree at the edge of the churchyard. As a shy guy, I couldn't just walk up and introduce myself, so I threw the football at her! It bounced off her head. Now was my opportunity to go over, apologize, and introduce myself. Pretty smart move, I thought.

Over the following days, we took every opportunity to slip away from our parents and meet. I had never had the nerve to talk to a girl, and now I was spending every possible moment with one. Wearing her Sunday-go-to-meeting outfit, flowered cap, and gloves, she looked like an angel. And when she twirled around, her dress flew out, and I could see her knees—my imagination ran wild. It was exhilarating! Before the conference concluded, we professed our love for one another and were determined to meet during the coming winter.

## SHADOWS COME AT MIDNIGHT

The return to our family home in the backwoods was a long, two-hour drive. I was one lonely guy. To occupy me between chores and schoolwork, I spent my time with animals. Both domestic and wild. I had a knack for training dogs to pull the water sleigh, move cattle, and carry my books to and from the daily bus that took us to school in the nearby town. I also befriended deer, skunks, and rabbits. But I could only think of the *what-ifs* of my budding romance with the goddess.

Christmas came and went. Our family shared meals with the neighbors, went on hayrides, played hockey on the pond, and rode bicycles over the frozen drifts. There was no television, and my parents placed severe restrictions on using the old Motorola radio. Most evenings, we played board games such as Crokinole, Snakes-and-Ladders, or a new game called "Sorry." But my mind was always looking for ways to get to the city and see Janice. So, late one January evening, I made the fateful decision to go to Winnipeg and rekindle our romance. There was one problem—I didn't have a car.

My first thought was to hike down to the highway—about five miles west—and hitch a ride to the city. With the snow covering the road and the temperature dipping well below zero, that thinking mode lasted only until the lane's end—too cold, too windy, and too much snow. So off to the neighbors'. Thinking I could knock on their door and borrow their car for the evening, I created a story that I thought believable, which might give them the reason to loan me their brand-new 1964 Meteor sedan. It was the community's showpiece: V8 motor, power windows, reverse-slant rear window, and automatic transmission. That would impress Janice!

As I walked up to their long driveway, I realized what time it was, just after ten p.m. The lights were off, and they had gone to bed. I'd hate to wake them up. What now? Perhaps I could just borrow it—they probably wouldn't mind. Maybe they wouldn't even know I took it. So, on that cold winter night, I made a decision that would change the direction of my life. I sneakily made my way to the machine shop where they stored the car at night and opened the double-wing doors. There it was in all its splendor: baby-blue body, white top, and loads of chrome. I slipped behind the wheel.

Ensuring the lights weren't on, I started the car. That big V8 engine sounded like a freight train, and I was shaking by the time I pulled it out of the shed. I was sure that lights would pop on at any time, and George would come running with a shotgun. Everyone had guns in our neck of the woods, and I could just imagine the owner's state of mind seeing his prize vehicle heading down the road. He would shoot me without a thought. I had just stolen his car.

Safely onto the road, I turned on the lights and headed for the big city. It was an exciting adventure. Here I was, seventeen years old, driving a brand-new car, tank three-quarters full, heater turned high, tunes belting from the radio, and on my way to everlasting love. I was cool before cool was in style.

I drove carefully on the snow-covered roads. I didn't want to get George's car in a wreck. At the intersection where the narrow county road met the main highway, I came to a full stop, signaled a right turn, and headed for Winnipeg. I had the address but didn't have a clue how to find my way to her house. Still, I recalled that she had said she lived in the St. James part of the city during our chats, so all I had to do was find the general area and start my search. By that time, it was after midnight.

Street after street and avenue after avenue, I drove. I was searching for that elusive address. Increasingly, I was becoming discouraged. What if she had given me the wrong address? What if I misinterpreted the name of the area where she lived? And, even if I found the house, how would I wake her up without alerting her parents? I was near panic.

At last, just after two a.m., I found it. A small bungalow set back from the street. Wide porch with a shoveled walkway. I was here.

I crept up one side of the house, then the other, searching for her bedroom. Peering in the windows one at a time, it never crossed my mind that being a peeping tom was also a criminal offense. Oh, well. What I didn't know couldn't hurt me, I guess. One window was completely closed off with heavy curtains, so on to the next. The final window had frilly curtains, and there was just a crack in the middle I could peek through. I still didn't know if I had the right one but had to take a chance. I tapped on the glass.

After the third tap of the increasing loudness of my knuckles on the window, a hand reached up and pulled back the curtains. It was Janice. I had found my love. I must have looked like a ghost from a nightmare, dressed in my parka, felt boots, and a face covered in frost. I had planned to hitchhike and dressed for spending a lot of time on the side of the road.

I smiled, wiped the frost from my face, and gave a little wave. My dream girl recognized me, slid the window open, and just stared. With words of uncompromising clarity, I was rebuffed, rejected, and sent on my way. I never heard a Christian swear like that before.

Our romance was over.

# CHAPTER TWO

The journey home was long, my mind in confusion. *Why had she rejected me? How could this happen? Was it because I was a farm kid, and she was from the city? Maybe it was the way I dressed or the clumsy way I had knocked on her window. I thought it was romantic!* I drove away, accepting that I had built a dream on nothing but a figment of my imagination. But now a new worry. What to do about the stolen car?

The wind had picked up, and the blowing snow was beginning to obscure the road as I left the big city behind. By the time I passed through the small town closest to home, it was just after four a.m. I saw that the gas gauge was now less than a quarter tank, and there was still a way to go. But I believed I could make it with the remaining fuel and maybe slip the car back into the shed before anyone woke up. I settled back for the last leg of my trip, turned the heater up another notch, and pumped up the music. The night had not been a total waste. I had learned a lesson, driven a stolen car, and been on an adventure.

Lights shining in the farmyards at the ends of driveways were the only signs of life. I was alone. The warmth of the car and the country tunes on the radio settled my thoughts as I approached the intersection leading to my home. But now, parked at the cross-roads, was a police car. He was facing in my direction, so I would have to pass him. No problem. I'd keep my cool, give him a wave, and continue. As I passed, he glanced up from his paperwork. I smiled, gave him a friendly gesture, and kept heading on my way. In my rear-view mirror, I saw him turn his car to follow me. It didn't cross my mind to try to outrun him. But I did know that if he was after me and not on his way to a more urgent call, I was in deep trouble.

Yup, within a few minutes, the roof light on his car lit up, and I knew my night was about to take a wrong turn. I flipped my signal and pulled to the side of the road. He was alone and walked confidently and with a purpose to my window. I lowered the glass.

There he stood. Fur hat, blue parka rimmed with gold trim, gloves, and a flashlight shining in my face. "Good evening, young man. Where are you headed?"

"Home," I replied, my voice shaking.

"Can I see your driver's license, registration, and insurance?"

I dug through my wallet and produced my license. Burrowing through the glove box and looking above the visors, I couldn't find the ownership documents.

"Whose car is it?" he asked, taking a step back.

"My neighbor's."

"Do they know you have it?"

"I . . . I don't; I don't think so," I stammered.

He didn't say anything for a couple of minutes, just looked at me.

Finally, he reached forward, grasped the handle, and opened the door. "Come on back to my car," he said, motioning to the patrol vehicle parked behind me. I rolled up the window, stepped out, and followed him.

"Hop in the front seat," he motioned to the far side. I moved along the front of the black-and-white car and opened the passenger door. I had expected to be handcuffed and put in the back seat, but I didn't question his directions.

It was the first time I had been in a police car. It was not what I got to know and use many years later, but to a seventeen-year-old, the lights and switches on the dash looked like something from a spaceship. There were two radio microphones and a metal panel of buttons with stickers: roof light, fender light, siren, and two unmarked toggles.

I was surprised that the car wasn't more modern. There was no AM/FM radio. It had a standard transmission and just crank-up windows. It also had only two front doors—no back ones. It was dark outside, but the officer kept the headlights on, so the dash was lit and, it was warm inside.

He began the conversation with an easy question. "So, tell me about yourself and how come you're out here at this time of night."

I told him about my trip to Winnipeg, about Janice, about being rejected. Although I didn't burst out crying, the retelling of the past few hours brought home the reality of the situation I was in, and I certainly felt like bawling my eyes out.

"You've told me why you're out here tonight, but you haven't told me about yourself. What's going on?"

With that question, I opened up. I told how my mom was a schoolteacher; my dad worked odd jobs around the county, I had three brothers, and how my sister had died when I was little. I couldn't stop talking.

When I mentioned that I was held back a grade in school because I was a slow learner, he responded with a surprising comment. "So was I. What do you do to keep from believing that?"

That opened another floodgate, stuff I had never told anyone before. About my animals, about taking off into the bush for hours and hours—just to be by myself. My feelings of loneliness, even though I had three brothers and great parents. I didn't have any friends. How I believed I would never amount to anything because I was dumb.

He chuckled. "Well, whatever you believe about yourself, you'll become. If you think you'll never make anything of yourself, you won't. If you don't make friends, you will never have any. It's up to you."

He talked about character and about being a man. About honesty, hard work, getting along with people. Loyalty and compassion.

I don't know if he was giving me tips or relaying how he handled his own life. Maybe a bit of both, but I took it all in. I was fascinated.

He leaned back against the seat and studied me. "Look for what you can't do, are afraid of doing, or that other people say you can't do. Then go ahead and do it anyway."

We talked for over an hour. That wisdom, dispensed in the middle of nowhere on a cold winter night in a police car, has carried me through many a tough and trying time.

He glanced at his watch. "Well, I think it's time you took that car back where you found it." With that, he reached across me and opened the door. My time was up. He never mentioned the stolen car.

I climbed back into the Meteor and headed for home. I was shaking. *Why hadn't he arrested me and put me in reform school or something?* I would never know.

I killed the lights and turned the car into the yard I had left five hours earlier. I cautiously backed the vehicle into the enclosure and turned off the ignition. I had gotten away with it! I was thrilled.

Suddenly, the ceiling light of the old shed came on. And there stood George with an ax in his hands. Oh boy, was he some ticked off. Someone had stolen his new car, and now he had caught the thief. And it was me.

George was a German immigrant, built square with a massive chest and piercing eyes. He had a reputation for rough and tumble fights. I was in for a beating at the very least, and maybe even death. I just sat there.

I had forgotten that George was a dairy farmer and got up early to milk the cows. And now he had me. As I stepped from the car, he recognized me and lowered the ax.

"MacInnes," he said. "Whatever is to become of you?"

"Mr. Bensmiller," I replied. "I'm going to be a Mountie."

# CHAPTER THREE

The day I turned nineteen, I went to the local RCMP detachment and submitted my application. The timing was perfect. They were recruiting young, single men, physically fit, and they needed only a Grade Ten education. And I could ride a horse. After two medical examinations and three interviews, I was brought into a formal office and stood ramrod straight in front of a commissioned officer. He gave me a well-worn Bible that I held in my right hand. Then, in a solemn voice, he read from three separate cards.

The first reading was the Oath of Allegiance:

> *Do you solemnly swear that you will be faithful and bear true allegiance to Her Majesty Queen Elizabeth the Second, Queen of Canada, her heirs, and successors according to the law, so help you, God?*

I answered, "I do so swear," and lightly kissed the Bible.

He picked up the second card and read the Oath of Office:

> *Do you solemnly swear that you will faithfully, diligently, and impartially execute and perform the duties required of you as a member of the Royal Canadian Mounted Police? That you will well and truly obey and perform all lawful orders and instructions that you receive, without fear, favor, or affection of or toward any person, so help you, God?*

For the second time, I answered, "I do so swear," and touched the Bible with my lips.

I had anticipated both the first and second oaths, but there was still another. The Oath of Secrecy:

> *"Do you solemnly swear that you will keep absolutely secret all knowledge and information of which you may become possessed through your position with the Royal Canadian Mounted Police; that you will not, without due authority in that behalf, discuss with members of the force, or any other person, either by word or by letter, any matter which may come to your notice through your employment with the Royal Canadian Mounted Police, so help you, God?"*

And, for the third time, I responded and kissed the Bible. "I do so swear."

He then stepped forward and held out his hand. As I took it, he said, "You are now a constable in the Royal Canadian Mounted Police. Welcome."

He handed me a thick package. "This is your train ticket to the training center in Regina—Depot Division. There is also a list of items and clothing you need to take and some general information. Your train leaves at four-fifteen p.m., next Tuesday. Be on it."

And with those words, I became a member of the RCMP.

I was two hours early for the train. I didn't want to take any chances and somehow miss it. But promptly at four-fifteen, I was guided aboard by the conductor. Dressed in a suit and tie, I carried my one suitcase with all the items listed. It seemed like a short list. Just the basics itemized. Underwear, some socks, a couple of shirts, jeans, envelopes, stamps for letters home, and a topcoat to wear when I was off the training depot. And, of course, a second suit.

The conductor guided me through several cars, then opened a narrow door into a roomette. It was a complete setup. The room contained a bed, toilet, small desk, overhead rack for luggage, and a chair to look out the window at the passing scenery. I had never had that kind of sophisticated treatment before, and when he handed me a chit for dinner in the dining car, I thought then that this RCMP thing was going to be a walk in the park.

We traveled through the night. My nervous anticipation had been set aside by the royal treatment I was receiving on the train. The sound of the wheels clacking on the tracks and the sway of the sleeper car gave me one of the best rests I had in weeks.

I was jolted awake by a furious banging on the door of the roomette. I groggily scrambled out of bed to open the door. I thought maybe the train was on fire! I swung the door open to find a Mountie standing there. Although he didn't look much older than me, the sight of his rigid stance and perfectly tailored uniform told me that this was someone I shouldn't treat lightly or with any disrespect. "Get out of bed, rab!" he yelled. "Your life of luxury is over!" He had my full attention.

But he kept screaming at me. "Hurry up, get your stuff, straighten your tie, your boots look like shit, have you shaved yet, or are you too young to grow whiskers?" The insults just kept coming as I scrambled to get dressed and re-pack my luggage.

He marched me down the aisle of the train car and out onto the platform. There, standing shaking in the early morning chill were eight other recruits, baggage piled beside them; I was the last one to fall into line. And in front of this ragged band of rookies stood three other perfectly dressed Mounties. They gave not a smile, nod, or any recognition that we were even human.

"Down on your bellies!" one of them yelled. The nine of us lowered ourselves to the ground.

"Not good enough! Back to your feet, and this time when I tell you to drop to your bellies, YOU WILL DROP!"

The platform of the train station was wet and covered in mud from a recent late-spring snowfall. After fifty "to your feet, drop to your bellies" repetitions, we were covered in mud and near exhaustion.

"Wait till the corps sergeant major gets a look at this piss-poor bunch of recruits. He'll ship you all home, and you'll live in shame for the rest of your lives. Now pick up your so-called 'luggage' and fall-in."

None of us rabble had ever "fallen in," stood at attention, or marched as a group, so it was a motley cluster of dispirited men that climbed aboard the bus for the short journey to the training center. There were thirty-two of us in R-65/66 Troop, and we'd arrived at Depot from every part of Canada. If the instructor cadre intended to break us, they did an outstanding job. We were not given uniforms for the first couple of weeks; instead, we had to march everywhere in our *mufti* or civilian clothes. We learned how to march in unison and cadence. "By the left—quick march!" Shouted out, those words became the dominant sound in our lives. Arms swung shoulder high, fingers curled with thumb forward and thumbnail toward the sky. If we carried anything, such as books or a file, we would hold them rigidly down the seam of the left leg, arm stiff, eyes forward, chin lifted, chest out.

For the first while, as the "Junior Troop," we were *batboys* to senior troop members. We did their laundry, polished their boots, made their beds, and ironed their shirts. But they were also our mentors, giving tips on how to survive the harsh environment of Depot. We learned to use soap to enhance the ironed creases in our gym shorts and use the bottom of a hot spoon to smooth out the pebbles on our boot toe caps and give them a deep shine. A woman's pantyhose was better than a chamois for the final buffing of the gloss. They taught us how to roll our socks, hang our clothes, and make our bunks "the RCMP way," with hospital corners and the blankets tight enough to bounce a coin off. We weren't allowed to walk on the sidewalks. At mealtimes, we had to sit at the farthest tables from the cafeteria line.

## SHADOWS COME AT MIDNIGHT

It was a grueling six months. Days spent in swimming classes, equitation, stable duties, marching as a troop, and dreary hours of classroom learning. By nightfall, we were exhausted. Recruits who were more senior had the task of "night guard duty." The duties entailed a patrol of the stables and a check on the horses. The tour also included the various "secure" areas, such as the administrative buildings and the morgue. A part of the night-guard responsibilities was patrolling the barracks—particularly those that housed the junior troops.

It was a significant breach of discipline to leave so much as a speck of dust, an open book, or anything else that was not regimental on a desk when you hit the sack. The night guard would shake the rookie awake and have him stand at attention at the foot of his bed.

"What is your name?" he would ask. Then would follow a series of other questions, each one designed to force you fully awake. "What is the full name of your parents? Why did you join the RCMP if you're going to be this disrespectful of the uniform? Name all thirty-two members of your troop in alphabetical order." The questions came fast, with little time to respond. A missed answer always resulted in push-ups in the middle aisle as you struggled to regain some semblance of alertness.

The favorite question always seemed to be, "Recite the serial number of your revolver." To this day, I still remember it—C-244632. Smith and Wesson .38 Special.

But it wasn't only the night guard that interrupted sleep patterns. On at least a monthly basis, a member of the drill instructor team would usually trip the fire alarm around two a.m. The troop had a maximum of three minutes to be in troop formation on the parade square in front of the barracks. It was three floors down, and we all had to be dressed the same way and lined up in regular order. Coming from a dead sleep with alarms screaming, dressing alike, and hitting the stairs at a run, was an incredible challenge.

The penalty for being tardy or mixing uniform with the mufti, or not being in identical dress, was always ten laps of the enormous parade square at double time. It was an almost impossible task for thirty-two men to dress the same in the middle of the night.

But one night, we came up with a plan. And it was a good one!

The next time the alarm sounded, we scrambled into our pre-determined dress order. We were down on the parade square in two minutes and twelve seconds. A new record!

The drill instructor began to laugh uncontrollably. There stood an entire troop, lined up in regimental order, dressed in nothing but running shoes, jockstraps, raincoats, and Stetsons. No pants, no shirts, no ties—and no underwear. Were there consequences for our innovative action? You bet! This time, it was *twenty* laps of the square in the dead of night. We never pulled that stunt again.

Pursuit driving was a blast as we moved at speeds we always dreamed of, in and out of ditches, learning how to control a car in wet and dangerous conditions.

Lectures on RCMP history, first aid, criminal law, migratory bird regulations, Parliament functions, and dozens of other subjects filled our days, and homework filled our evenings. We were allowed two passes until eleven-thirty p.m. each week and a pass till one a.m. to pursue our social lives off base. A phone call to the Grey Nuns Nurse Training Center always garnered a compatible group to party with, or a faction would head down to the 4th Dimension Night Club to enjoy some light jazz.

Everyone in Regina knew we were Mounties-in-training. Our haircuts, high and tight, were the first sign, but wearing a suit and tie while off-Depot was the second. To our embarrassment and the citizens' enjoyment, the policy was to walk in lock-step. It might look great on the parade square, but the main-street sidewalks of downtown Regina? Not so much!

The physical part of the training was challenging. Hours spent in the pool, swimming until your arms ached. Marching in tight formation and watching troopmates fall from exhaustion. Five-mile runs in the early morning and night-guard duty every third weekend. But we became a troop. Although the training was unbelievably tough, the collected strength of thirty-two men living and learning together created bonds that still exist.

# CHAPTER FOUR

The RCMP's long-standing tradition was that a member was tough, strong, above the common man, and able to handle it all. If you couldn't do that, you were unworthy of the uniform. We memorized the details of the "March West" from Fort Garry, Manitoba, to Fort Macleod in southern Alberta and the dangers, starvation, and challenges the North-West Mounted Police faced and overcame. We committed to memory the skills and bravery of Sergeant-Major Steele, and the one-person escort of Sitting Bull into Canada was a model of courage and self-confidence.

The walls of the dining hall displayed dozens of paintings. A lone RCMP member with his dog team, high in the Arctic, or on his horse facing down a grizzly bear. These were the men who were to be our heroes. We had to live up to those expectations.

For some of us, a terrifying part of the training was swimming. On the first day, the instructors lined us up in regimental order at the pool's deep end. One by one, we approached the edge and were asked the question, "Can you swim?"

The corporal in charge of the pool stood at the side with a long pole. If you answered, "Yes, Corporal, I can," he told you to jump in the pool (it was twelve feet deep) and swim to the other side. The instructor watched you do so and put a little tick beside your name. If you said, "No, Corporal, I can't swim," he told you to jump in the pool anyway.

Over half the troop could not swim but had to prove their non-swimmer status to enter the novice class. After you flailed around and came close to drowning, the corporal would extend his pole and pull you to the side. If he believed you were faking it, he would ignore your screams until you went under for the third time. It was ironic that you didn't have to prove you knew how to swim—you had to prove you *didn't* know how to swim. By the end of the training, every troop member could pass the Bronze Medallion from the Royal Life Saving Society. Some achieved the coveted Award of Merit in swimming. Still, others succeeded in gaining SCUBA certification. They pushed us hard.

A challenging and often brutal sport was the RCMP version of water polo. All thirty-two recruits were in the pool; half were wearing bathing caps, and half were bare-headed. Yes, there were goal-nets, but that was secondary to the aim of the game. The objective was simple—keep the ball away from the opposing team. There were no rules. You could throw the ball to a teammate, hold it underwater to hide it, or grasp it in a death-grip and try to make it to the goal-line. And, if a member of the opposing team was holding it, you could do whatever it took to free the ball from his grasp. Bloody noses, scaped and bruised arms, and sprained wrists were all a part of the contest. After an hour of water-based unarmed combat, the corporal would declare a draw.

The training was exhausting, mind-numbing, and, at times, even terrifying. But, for me, the one bright spot in the weekly syllabus was working with the horses. The equitation program began in the second week of our training. As with all things RCMP, it had its own "system." The riding instructor introduced us to the tack we would be using for the duration of our training—saddle, halter, bridle, reins, and of course, the broom. Half of the troop would be assigned early-morning stable duties, while the other half consigned to sweep the parade square. Whichever section allocated had to be cleaned to perfection, and every broom-stroke had to be in perfect unison with the other fifteen men in your half-troop. It must have been quite a sight to the uninitiated—rows of men with push-brooms, chanting a ditty and pounding the brooms into the cement aisles in a deafening cadence. Full manure carts tipped into a central pile would later be taken out of the barn to the expanding stack on the west side.

The troop operated as a single unit—everything in unison, and everything done under the demanding eye of a riding instructor. Should one of the recruits slack off, complain, or draw the instructor's attention, everyone would suffer. A favorite penance was to bring the horses into the arena and stand them in two rows. Then, one by one, each member would do a series of "over and under's," climbing over one horse's back, then crawling under the next and repeating until all thirty-two horses were either over'ed or under'ed. It was exhausting and dirty!

Because all had to suffer for the actions of one, retribution against the slacking individual was inevitable. It was either a penalty of horse-troughing or shit-dipping. The other men would tackle the miscreant, drop him into the horse trough, and hold him underwater until he panicked. Eventually, he would rise from the water trough, offer his apologies, and swear he would never do that again. If shit-dipped, he would be buried to his neck in the manure pile, along with his saddle, bridle, and grooming equipment. It always occurred just as chores were finishing, and we had thirty minutes to shower and change for breakfast. Seldom did the shit-dipper make the bell. But, more importantly, the wrongdoer would never repeat his error.

The twice-per-week training sessions were each a half-day in length. During the first month, we were not allowed to have stirrups. We learned how to "post" the trot without aids. It was a difficult time. Until we toughened up, each session ended with blood running down the inside of our thighs, and our knees rubbed raw from the constant friction against the rough cotton breeks we wore.

We learned quickly to purchase women's silk underwear to help limit the chafing and put Vaseline gobs on the inside of our knees.

Each evening before our scheduled equitation session, riders reported to the stables to clean and oil tack. It became a social time for the guys as we got to know each other better, learning our pasts, why we'd joined the force, and what we hoped for in the future. As well, plans were formed for excursions "off Depot" during the upcoming weekends. What groups to try to link up with, whether we had time to go to Qu'Appelle Valley on a road trip or spend the day in barracks. Members who were struggling with obscure points of law (such as *Authority and Power of Part Fourteen Magistrates*) were tutored by those who had mastered the incomprehensible section.

All riding instructors were former members of the Musical Ride—some were also instructors for the ride, so the demand for perfection was always present. Each equine training period began with grooming the horse. We would place a measure of oats in the manger and, as the horse ate, would use the curry comb, flicker brush, mane and tail rake, and hoof pick to prepare the horse for inspection. It was a sin to have a speck of dust on the horse or a hair out of place. Any error was cause for the assignment of extra duties to be performed that same evening. These could range from standing guard at the morgue to polishing the garbage cans in the drill hall with a toothbrush. "Character development," they called it.

After the riding instructor inspected our horses, we could lead them into the arena. Lined up in two rows by regimental numbers, we learned the basics of mounting. First, stand on the horse's left side, right hand on the rein and bodies at full military attention. On the command "Stand to your horses," we would step forward, turn to face the horse head-on, and place both hands on the reins just behind the bit—still at attention. Then a further command of "to your horses," and we would move our left hand to the left rein, turn, step forward, and stand with our bellies toward the saddle with our left hands moving up the rein toward the saddle. On the command

"Prepare to mount," all thirty-two men would place their left feet in the stirrup, grasp the saddle's cantle, and remain standing until the final command: "Mount." Should any rider be out of sync with the other members or fail to follow the instructions correctly, the process would continue until perfected.

Moving in the formation and copying the Musical Ride moves, I learned how to ride a horse the "Mountie Way." Gone were the days of relaxing in the saddle and working cattle. But I could sit the transitions, jump on Suicide Alley, and do a correct lead change. Other troop mates weren't so lucky. Many had never been on a horse before they arrived at Depot.

As we drew closer to graduation, or "Pass Out," there was an increase in the equitation drills' complexity and faster movements. If you lost your hat during a move, you paid twenty-five cents. If you fell off or thrown off, the cost increased to a dollar. The instructor's goal was to see thirty-two men on the ground during training. To that end, they brought in two "remounts" from Fort Macleod. These were green-broke horses that had some basic training but could be unpredictable and were always on the edge of being out of control. Then off to Suicide Alley for a run down the jumps.

At the final jump, the mount ridden by the other member who had managed to stay aboard for the past five-and-a-half months, twisted to the side, bucked high and wide, and Brian became airborne. Now I was the only one remaining who had not hit the ground. So, off to the willows!

The willow stand was about an acre in size and crisscrossed with old logs, thatches of impenetrable red willow, and a few faint trails. We were doing well, keeping up with the more experienced and skilled horses ahead of us. But then came the infamous mud hole! My remount, Erant, had a sound mind and lots of *try*, but a minimal experience. I slowed him down and started into the mud pit. He balked. I gave him the chance to figure it out on his own, then gave him a touch of the spur. Big mistake! He snorted, pawed the mud, then reared back. Usually, I would shift my weight forward, and a horse would feel the shift and lower its front end down to the ground. But not this time. Erant continued to rear higher, finally coming over backward and pinning me to the ground. I felt an intense pain in my left elbow. I struggled out from beneath him, and he scrambled back to his feet.

"OK, MacInnes, you owe the fund a dollar," came a bellow. "Now, get back in the saddle and join the others—and clean your uniform—you look a mess."

I started to explain that I'd broken my arm. "I told you to get back in the saddle! If you're looking for sympathy, you won't find it here." He spouted one of his favorite sayings: "If you're looking for sympathy, you need a dictionary. You'll find it between shit and syphilis, but you won't find it with me." I painfully crawled back onto the saddle and continued the ride.

And so, I finished my basic training with an injury. The doctor who examined me late that same afternoon placed the cast from mid-bicep to wrist but formed it in such a way that there was still a slight bend to the elbow so I could march with my troop for the graduation ceremonies in two weeks.

As we approached the final day of training, we completed a form expressing our wishes for three areas we would like to police. We could not go to our home province, so I selected the Maritimes, the Lower Mainland of British Columbia, and the Arctic. They sent me to Alberta.

The graduation process was an incredible experience. My parents had traveled from Manitoba to be a part of the celebration. Up at five-thirty a.m. to get ready. Throughout the day, we gave displays of swimming, physical training, first aid, and horsemanship. At the Drill Hall, the commanding officer presented us with our Badges of Office and Warrants of Authority.

The Pass Out Parade was a demonstration of precision foot-drill maneuvers. We had practiced the various movements for weeks, and it was flawless. Then, marching through the north gates, coming to a halt, and throwing our Stetsons in the air—we made it! Although some of us were awkward in foot drill, some nearly drowned during swimming, and others struggled with the academics, we were one of the few troops to make it through training with all thirty-two members still present.

We made it!

## CHAPTER FIVE

It was late summer as we headed out from Regina to our assigned detachments in Alberta. I had bought a 1958 Chevy the week before graduation, so I took three of the recruits. Two other cars with rookies aboard followed behind as we made our way west.

The drive to Edmonton took about ten hours, the conversations full of words of excitement. We were on our way to being full-fledged Mounties in one of the fastest-growing areas of Canada. The oil boom was beginning, and the industry was ramping up; rig workers were filling every motel and hotel in Alberta, and policing increased. The future looked bright, indeed.

We approached the imposing Grierson Hill complex with a mixture of awe and apprehension. The compound had been built in 1912 to house the original North-West Mounted Police headquarters and continued to be the center of command for the entire province of Alberta, known as "K" Division. The magnificent limestone buildings were situated on the North Saskatchewan River's highest bank and resembled a castle and grounds from medieval times. A parade square formed the center of the complex, with the structures facing inward.

During the 1950s, the force had renovated the basement into an underground garage for police vehicles. And the Edmonton Detachment located above the garage. Across the square, the Financial Services and Supply (FCSS) division handled the entire force's ongoing requirements in Alberta. The lower floors contained a tailor, saddlery, quartermaster, and even a barbershop—all holdovers from a plan originating from a military-garrison style.

Upon arrival, the officer commanding "K" Division met us and read out the assigned detachments list. From the nine of us posted to Alberta, the CO sent seven on to rural postings and retained two of us to perform tasks in the Edmonton region. This area included towns and villages in the surrounding countryside, some as far as fifty miles away.

Hauling our duffle bags, racks of uniform and civilian clothes, and a suitcase of personal items, we climbed the stairs to the second-floor barracks. It became the home where single men would live while assigned to general duties—sparsely equipped with a row of single cots and no dividing walls. Only a small desk, straight-backed chair, and wardrobe completed the furnishings. The quartermaster issued a pillow, sheets, and two wool RCMP-emblazoned blankets.

I was excited to begin my actual police patrols but found myself assigned as court security at the Alberta Court of Queen's Bench. There, I had to sit for all the sessions, wearing my full Red Serge uniform, Sam Browne belt with holstered revolver, handcuff pouch, and cross-strap. It was a sluggish start to my policing career. Some of the cases were interesting and kept my attention, but the ones involving white-collar crime or dealing with bankruptcies and commercial fraud were boring, at best. I often felt myself dozing off as the lawyers droned on and on, listing dozens of minutia points about cases decided decades previously that might apply to their argument. On the third day, I nodded off in the middle of a preliminary hearing involving a dispute between two business owners. My head dropped to my chest, and I started to snore.

"CONSTABLE!" That one word, spoken very loudly, very clearly, woke me from my precious few minutes of rest and brought me to my feet in rigid attention. "You will NOT sleep in my courtroom!" The presiding judge glared down at me from his bench as he scolded me. "Do you understand?"

"Yes, sir!" I responded in my best recruit voice. "I understand, and I apologize for my lapse. It will not happen again."

"See that it doesn't, or I will have you removed and replaced. You are here to add to the dignity of the court, and sleeping on the job does not fulfill that obligation in any way."

I was embarrassed and ashamed but determined never to fall asleep in court again. When the trial adjourned for the day, the judge called me into his chambers. I thought I was in for a dressing-down at best or that he would report me to my commanding officer for disciplinary action. I was surprised and somewhat relieved when he motioned for me to take a seat across from his desk.

He had taken off his black robe and was wearing a T-shirt, jeans, and running shoes. He leaned back and put his feet up on the desk, and sighed. "I know some of the cases are complex and maybe even a bit boring, but they are all important," he began. "And at times, the lawyers get wordy and wander off into some wilderness of their imaginings. However, it is my court, and I need you awake and alert. You are there representing the Queen, and I think she would be a bit disappointed to see you with your head on your chest and snoring."

I nodded, "Yes, sir, you are right. Again, I apologize."

"I know the room is warm, you're in full uniform, probably don't get enough rest, and yes, some of the lawyers droning on can lull even the best of us to nod off, so I understand."

We continued our conversation for another half-hour. The judge asked me about my family, Depot training, and why I had chosen to become a Mountie. I didn't dare tell him about my theft of a car—the statute of limitations was still in effect and, to put it bluntly, I was scared spitless that if he knew the details, I would end up in the prisoner's box rather than being a guard beside it.

He put his feet down and leaned forward. "I don't know why the force gave you this particular assignment—maybe to give you some development, maybe as a form of punishment, or maybe there was just a spot that needed filling. Whatever the reason, you are here now and will probably be here every day until this session is over. You will find some interesting cases that hold your attention and interest and some that bore you to tears. But you can learn something from every trial if you pay attention."

I could only nod in response.

"You can learn the difference between homicide and murder" (*that* intrigued me!) or the fact that we do not have any anti-slavery laws in Canada. Each hearing is unique and has, within its prosecution and defense, some intriguing point of law. Look for it and learn."

I gave a crooked grin. "But I have to stay awake, right?"

The judge chuckled. "Yes, I'm afraid you have to stay awake. And, sometimes, even I have trouble keeping my attention on the arguments presented. If you watch, the lawyers also struggle to be alert at times."

"You know," he continued, "whenever I have to do a job that I don't really like, or find boring but know I have to do, I just say to myself, 'I can do anything for fifteen minutes.' Then," he added, "if the task is longer, I just repeat for another fifteen minutes."

He dismissed me from his office, and the court bailiff escorted me back to the courtroom to take my position for the next hearing.

That judge became a mentor of mine, and over the next twenty-plus years, I would have the opportunity to have a coffee with him and visit. He would often tell me things I needed to hear—not the things I wanted to hear. But I've carried that first conversation throughout my life. Whether it was doing point duty at an accident scene or shoveling manure in the stables, I go back to that statement: *I can do anything for fifteen minutes.*

The court sitting lasted for five weeks. It was boring at times, intriguing at other times, but I never again went to sleep. And I learned that, in a historical sense, homicide was the killing of a human being, and a murder was the killing of an Englishman. And each had different penalties. Years later, I had the honor of being on a committee led by Heather Forsyth, solicitor general of Alberta, to enact the first law in Canada to address the trafficking and modern-day slavery of children. The Protection of Children Involved in Prostitution Act was passed into law by the legislature.

★ ★ ★

"No Red Serge on Monday." The staff sergeant spoke those magic words as I walked into the office late Friday afternoon. "You are now assigned to general patrol duties. Report to the parade room before the day shift on Monday. The corporal will assign you to a senior constable who will show you the ropes. Listen to him."

With those words, my real career in law enforcement was about to begin.

# CHAPTER SIX

I spent the weekend in high anticipation. After five weeks in uniform, sitting in a sweltering courtroom listening to a bunch of lawyers, I was about to go out on patrol! I must have polished my boots a half-dozen times. With my uniform trousers ironed, I put sharp creases in my shirts and dusted my forage cap. My Sam Browne was gleaming, and I installed new batteries in my flashlight. I was ready.

"Hi, I'm Donny Pearson." The young Mountie reached forward to shake my hand. He was clean-shaven and sported the short regulation haircut. I shook his hand as we took our seats in the parade room and waited for the corporal to enter.

He grinned. "It looks like we'll be partners for the next few months or so. I'll show you around. I've only been on the street for about three years, but they gave me the job of being your training officer. Usually, they give these assignments to the older guys, but there's been a lot of recruits added to the roster, so you get me."

"Sounds good," I replied. "What do we do today?"

"I'll show you the district and let you get familiar with it. We're patrolling the area west of the city, so that's where we'll spend the next while. It covers a fairly large territory, and there are some small towns, a couple of reserves, and lots of back roads."

Donny introduced me to several others in the room. Although we had met in passing a few times as I had been driven back and forth to my court assignments, this was the first time I would be out on the street with them.

"Attention!" All twelve of us scrambled to our feet and stood rigidly at attention. The corporal made his rounds, assessing each of us. He looked carefully at our uniforms, checked our notebooks, and, on several occasions, had a member remove his handcuffs for inspection. Satisfied, he pronounced, "At ease. Take your seats."

We settled in behind the old school desks as he passed out "hot sheets" to each officer. The sheets included recently stolen cars, descriptions of individuals wanted for questioning, and core information on incidents that had happened overnight. He then went through the group handing out file folders with subpoenas, minor warrants, summonses to be served, and notifications to be delivered.

"Here's yours, MacInnes," he said, handing me a thick file. "These have all been diary-dated in the logbook, so have them done before the due dates, or you can ask for an extension if needed. But don't ask for extensions on the summonses or subpoenas. You must serve them at least three days before the court dates." With those words, he passed on to the next member as I glanced through the folder. *Maybe patrolling isn't quite as exciting as I thought.*

"All right, guys, stay safe out there." With that admonition, we headed out on patrol.

Donny motioned me to follow, and he picked up a wooden box he had stored near the door. "I built it for the car," he said. "It holds my files, ticket book, flashlight, and the other stuff. I just set it on the seat between us, and it's my portable desk. I copied it from one of the older guys." I felt a bit under-equipped, holding just my flashlight and folder of files the corporal had given me.

"We'll grab a car and head out. You can drive, and I'll ride shotgun. That way, you can get a feel for the district, and I can kind of point out some of the key points as we go." He selected a key from the "assignment board" and swung open the basement garage door.

The patrol cars were all parked in rows, and Donny pointed to one near the second line. "This is ours." He tossed me the keys.

The car assigned was typical of others in the lineup. Black Plymouth Fury with the RCMP crest on the white front doors. Two-door sedan, 318 cubic inch V8, with a three-on-the-tree standard transmission. No AM/FM radio, air conditioning, power windows, or locks. An eight-inch gum-ball red light on the roof, a stoplight mounted on the right front fender, and a frame-mounted spotlight above and to the left of the steering wheel completed the needed equipment.

"Do a walk-around, and check all the lights, the oil, coolant, and the like." My partner made a circular motion indicating a full hike around the vehicle. "That way, you'll know if the previous shift did any damage to the car, the oil is low, or they didn't fill the tank before booking off."

I knew that the driver had to pay out of payroll deductions if anything happened to the car. I had heard of one guy that had failed to check the oil and blew the motor. He ended up paying over $1,000 for his mistake. I was too poor to take any chances.

I made the requisite inspections. Nothing out of the ordinary, but I did notice that our car had the new Firestone 500 tires. A significant improvement over the contract equipment we had in training.

I settled into the driver's seat as Donny slid into his. The driver's seat had been crushed down over the years by officers who were considerably heftier than me. While the suspension on the car itself was heavy-duty, the seats were not! The radio had only two channels. The "A" channel was for local transmission of detachment concerns. The "B" channel was for a more distant broadcast using a radio repeater station operated by the federal government, call-sign XJK-88. An aluminum dash-plate contained the switches that ran the siren, roof light, and fender-mounted stoplight. Pretty basic.

I tested the lights and siren, and so did the other members who were heading out. The confined space of the basement and the concrete walls created a loud noise. We could have all waited until we were out of the garage, but I think there was a perverse desire to annoy the administrative people working above us. It indeed infuriated the higher-ups, but they never seemed to stop us from doing so.

Then, up the ramp and onto the street. A quick left turn and we were heading west on Jasper Avenue, the main artery through downtown Edmonton. Traffic was light but steady as we left the city to begin our tour of my new patrol area. I found it interesting that other cars would slow down when they spotted us, even if they were already doing the speed limit. A couple of truckers gave us a nod or a wave, and I felt good. I was in the job of my dreams.

The territory we were assigned to cover was huge. Small towns surrounded each side of the city, with a half-dozen located in our area alone. Also, there were five Indian reserves, nine "summer towns" located at various lakes through the region, and miles of highways and secondary roads. It was impossible to cover the entire district during a shift.

Donny directed me through the various places of interest or concern, such as bars, hotels, and party-spots located through the area. Several dance halls operated along the main highway, although they were closed during the day. But he pointed them out to me as places to check when on the night shift. I raised my concern that, as I was only nineteen and Alberta's legal drinking age was twenty-one, I couldn't check these places. He assured me that, although I couldn't go in them when I was off-duty, my warrant-card was enough authority for me to inspect them while on patrol. Through our tour, Donny pointed out several areas of concern, including a small twenty-four-hour service station/café, on Edmonton's outskirts.

## CHAPTER SEVEN

Due to a limited workforce and increased call-load, we took separate cars on patrol but remained partners over the next few weeks. We left the detachment simultaneously, usually met up for a coffee or lunch sometime during our shift, and put our cars away on conclusion. We had some great discussions. He told me how he had just married the love of his life and showed me a picture of her that he always carried in his wallet.

He would quiz me about *what-ifs*. What *if* you stop another officer for drunk driving—what do you do? What *if* you see an out-of-work father stealing a few groceries for his family—what do you do? What *if* you know of a child molester but can't secure the evidence for court? Donny wasn't looking for answers but rather to make me think of the broader (and often moral) issues we face as police officers.

We talked about fishing, sports, and how sadly the Edmonton Eskimos football team was doing this year. He was a fan of the Eskimos, but it sure didn't look like they would have a winning season. His second choice was the Saskatchewan Roughriders. They were having a good season, and if the Eskimos couldn't get the job done, maybe Saskatchewan could. The Championship Grey Cup would play in Vancouver on November 26th.

If assigned to the day or afternoon shifts, our focus would be on "the files." Serving summonses for court appearances or delivering witness subpoenas. As usual, there were a few arrest warrants that we carried as part of our caseload. Typically, they were for minor offenses such as failing to appear in court on a summons, not paying a fine, or lower-level crimes like shoplifting or theft of gasoline.

And on those shifts, we never wore our revolvers. We would only carry that piece of equipment for court duty or night shift. After all, we were Mounties!

We kept our sidearms in cubby holes in the office. Each officer had an assigned spot. There, he kept his revolver and five bullets. As part of our training, a loaded weapon always had an empty chamber under the firing pin just in case you dropped your sidearm and "lit one-off." Some officers didn't follow protocol but instead kept the empty slot to the left of the hammer. Their thinking was that if a suspect grabbed your weapon and went to fire it, the first trigger pull wouldn't hit a live round, and you would have time to wrestle him down. Within a few months, the CO abandoned the policy of not carrying your weapon while on duty or having anything less than fully loaded and ready.

As a one-person car, I felt the pressure of performing my duties, not just to the best of my ability, but to my superiors' implicit expectations and those of my partner out in the second car.

If you were going to call for back-up, it better be a critical call! Adhering to that unspoken policy would, on occasion, bring about some exciting and even dangerous situations.

On a bright autumn morning, I worked on my files and was determined to finish delivering the various subpoenas, summonses, and minor warrants before lunch. By about eleven-thirty, I was down to my last file—a summons for a man to appear before the Family Court for failing to pay child support. This document-serve should be an easy one.

The subject was living in a cheap motel on the outskirts of the city. When I went to the premises manager, I learned that the gentleman worked at a nearby construction site. So, off I went to finish up my last file.

As I turned onto the narrow dirt track leading toward the area under construction, I noted an old shack used as a field office.

Spotting a movement inside the small structure, I stopped to inquire about the man's whereabouts. An overweight man wearing bib overalls, a plaid shirt, and a hard hat came out to meet me. As per standard procedures, I gave my name and the fact that I needed to speak to an individual. I provided the guy's name, but not the purpose of my inquiry. The fellow in the overalls pointed down the trail to where several bulldozers and earthmovers were scraping topsoil off a large section of an open field. I got back into my car and headed toward the site. A sign indicated the construction of a new shopping center and cautioned that machinery was operating in the area.

As I got closer, I noted a Euclid Earthmover leave the site and travel down the roadway toward me. *Oh,* I thought, *the older man must have signaled the subject somehow, and he's coming to meet me! That's great!* I had stepped out of my car to meet him, and then I heard the colossal machine begin to accelerate. Maybe his motive for coming to meet me wasn't so great after all.

In a panic, I jumped back in the car, threw the shift into reverse, and stomped on the gas. It was still coming! Ripping backward down that narrow trail, being chased by a massive earthmover at over thirty miles per hour, all my *tough Mountie* training seemed trivial. I was in full retreat.

I don't think the site foreman heard my girlish screams as I was in my car racing backward, so maybe he just sensed that this scene was about to get very ugly. Whatever the reason, he waved me past the checkpoint and, as I whizzed by, pointed me in the direction of the staff parking lot. I skidded into the entrance, the front of my car slewing sideways. The scraper had to slow to make the sharp corner, and it gave me the chance to tuck in between the parked cars. I hoped that would give him pause to reconsider his actions. Maybe he came to his senses, or perhaps he was reluctant to demolish his co-workers' cars, but whatever the reason, he stopped, reversed, and headed back to the construction site.

I met up with Donny for lunch at the small café at the west end of our detachment area. Sometimes I'm prone to exaggerate a few details, but this time I didn't need to. That confrontation had scared the crap out of me! His response? He laughed! Not just a chuckle, but a full-blown, doubled over, coffee coming-out-his-nose, laugh! He then had me repeat it. I believe he wanted all the details precisely right to relate it to the guys at the barracks.

Later that same afternoon, Donny accompanied me back to the construction site. We parked our cars a distance away and waited. Eventually, our subject left his machine to log out of his shift and head for the parking lot. Without fanfare, we boxed his car with the two police cars, and I served him with the summons.

He told us his whole story. He had got behind in his child-support payments and had just started the new job so he could catch up on things. He still carried a massive debt from the divorce proceedings and was afraid that he would lose his job if he went to court. We decided not to charge him with trying to run me over. Donny explained how he could ask for additional time to pay and that he could call the site foreman to court to describe the job and how he was guaranteed to have the work for at least the next few months. He also clarified that Canada didn't have a debtors' prison anymore. He wouldn't go to jail—only lose a half-day in court.

"Certainly, better than a murder charge," my partner said as we turned to go.

"Sorry about that," the relieved man grinned. "I guess I wasn't thinking. Thanks for the break."

★ ★ ★

It was a real pleasure getting to meet the citizens of the area. With few exceptions, they welcomed us into their businesses and homes—a coffee, a home-made piece of pie, and, often, a note of appreciation. We would drop in at schools and amateur sporting events, visit farmers bringing in their crops from the fields, and sometimes look in on small businesses to say hi. While there was the rare critical call, most were minor.

Each Wednesday, we would check the duty-roster to determine our assignments for the following week. There was a regular rotation of duties, with members being assigned dayshift (eight to four), afternoons (four to midnight), or midnight to eight a.m. We saw that both of us were on the afternoon shift starting on Monday, November 21. Again, due to call-load and limited workforce, we were to patrol in one-man cars.

It was Grey Cup week, and, even on a Monday, the hotel bars were busy with televised events leading up to the big football game the following weekend. We checked parking lots for illegal drinking, broke up a few bar fights, and arrested a couple of drunks—nothing serious, just part of the job.

Late in the shift, we grabbed a quick break to chat before heading back to the detachment office, conclude our shift, and do the necessary paperwork. I did a final sweep of my assigned area near Devon's small riverside community, and Donny headed west on the highway to check on a few things before we went back to the garage.

I arrived at the detachment before he did and had put my car away and climbed the stairs to complete a couple of General Occurrence Reports. After finishing the necessary tasks, I went up to bed. Donny was still out there.

There had been a drunken fight at the Holly Esso in Winterburn, the small all-night service station/café on Edmonton's western edge. My partner was dispatched to the scene—alone. The fight was over when Donny got there. As he was about to leave, one of the participants returned and walked in, carrying a .303 rifle. He shot Donny.

I was asleep.

# CHAPTER EIGHT

I scrambled out of my warm bed in confusion and panic. *What happened? Did he say somebody shot Donny? What the hell was going on?*

Grabbing my uniform from where it hung in the closet, I struggled to put it on in my half-asleep state. Once I had got my shirt buttoned and Sam Browne belt around my waist, I ran for the stairs and down to the office. The place was a madhouse. Officers shouting back and forth, sergeants trying to get things organized, and cars and equipment dispatched. No one knew any details. We only knew that a police officer had been wounded and was now at the hospital in life-threatening condition.

Two-man car assignments were being made in a mad dash to get all personnel out on the road and looking for the suspect. We didn't have a clear picture of what was going on or who had shot Cst. Pearson. In the chaos, we didn't even have a proper description of the shooter, only that he was male, possibly an Aboriginal, and he had a rifle. Not much to go on, and only an urgent need to get out onto the roads and make our presence known. Maybe we would spot something suspicious and get lucky and catch the guy.

I spotted another officer, who held up a set of car keys and motioned me over with a wave of his hand. "We're going together; I'll drive," he yelled over the commotion of the office. "Stay right here, and I'll be back in a second."

He disappeared for a few moments, returning with a pump-action 12-gauge shotgun. I noted other officers were dashing out to their cars or upstairs to the barracks and returning with their rifles and shotguns. They weren't going to rely solely on their issued weapon if they had to confront the suspect. Officers grabbed revolvers from the office's pigeonholes, slid the bullets into the cylinder, and jammed their sidearms into their holsters.

Taking the stairs two at a time, we rushed to the basement and grabbed our assigned vehicle. Other two-man crews were scrambling into theirs, and the General Investigation Section officers, in plain clothes, were leaping into their unmarked cars. No one took the time to check the tires, oil, or vehicle body, hoping that the previous shift had done their part and left the cars adequately prepared.

The ramp leading out of the garage became a launchpad, as car after car raced up the incline, became airborne for a moment, then skidded and slid onto the street. Sirens screamed, lights flashed, and men in the front seat stared out the windshield with grim faces and angry eyes. Someone had shot a Mountie. Someone had shot my partner.

Dozens of police cars from the Edmonton City Police joined the search, and RCMP members from surrounding detachments united in a single-minded focus to find the shooter. Every back alley, parking lot, camping spot, dirt road, and construction site got searched. The radio dispatcher tried to keep things organized, but it was a momentous task. Information was sketchy as we still didn't know who the suspect was, nor did we have any description of his vehicle. But we were kept updated on Donny's condition—he was still alive.

My new partner was unfamiliar with the area, having patrolled Edmonton's east side in the Sherwood Park area. I directed him as best I could, checking the various side roads and lanes where a car could have hidden as the suspect made his escape. Often, we would head up a laneway, pound on the door of the farmhouse, and alert the occupants to watch for any stranger or unfamiliar vehicle coming into their farm.

We passed the scene where the shooting had taken place. The parking lot was packed with police vehicles. The Identification

Section was busy taking pictures, gathering evidence, and measuring distances. Members of the General Investigation Section were interviewing witnesses, and there was a police service dog and handler checking for any scent trail that might lead away from the café.

We didn't know if there might be a second suspect involved, so any car or pickup truck traveling with a single driver was pulled over and questioned. There were tense moments when a driver would be slow to respond to our lights and siren—*was this the one?* The radio chatter was busy with members giving their locations and reciting license numbers and descriptions. They stopped cars to check the occupants and often, not "clearing" from their call afterward. The XJK-88 dispatcher had a difficult time keeping track of all the activity taking place.

As we prepared to expand the search area in the early morning, the announcement came over the police radio. "The suspect has been arrested. All shift units return to regular duty; all other units return to detachments or barracks." No other details as to the name of the suspect, age, or ethnicity. We had no information about whether the suspect surrendered or it was a violent arrest.

My temporary partner and I returned to Grierson Hill to refuel and put the vehicle away. We were driving down the ramp when the dispatcher asked for a moment of silence.

At 2:15 a.m., November 22, 1966, Charles Hill murdered my partner.

We learned later that Donny had died shortly after being admitted to the hospital's emergency room, but the detectives kept that information off the airwaves. At that time, the Canadian Criminal Code made the killing of a police officer a hanging offense. The command center did not want Donny's death announced until the suspect had been captured. They believed that if the suspect knew that he had killed an officer, there would be a gun battle to arrest him. If he thought the officer was still alive, it would give the arresting officers a bit of room to negotiate a peaceful surrender.

We remained quiet as we completed our tasks and parked the car. Carrying our gear up the stairs, I began to cry. I had lost an incredible partner, mentor, and friend. The sense of loss was overwhelming.

The mood in the detachment was one of sadness and grief. We were stunned. Members stood around the office, gathering strength from each other—a brotherhood that had lost a family member. It was the first time we had faced our mortality for most of us, and we were unprepared for this revelation. Not once during basic training or at any in-service courses were we ever aware that this was a possibility we faced. Nor did it ever even enter our consciousness. We didn't know what to do.

A senior staff sergeant who'd commanded the search moved through the milling officers, patting a shoulder here, giving a quick hug there, or sometimes just a touch. He was trying to hold us together while struggling to keep his own emotions in check. We all huddled in the room, many still holding their rifles and shotguns, but none placed their service revolvers back into the cubbyholes. It was our security in a frightening time.

Tears were flowing unashamedly down faces, and there were low mutterings of frustration, anger, and uncertainty. *Why? Why did the guy have to shoot him? Did Donny have his weapon on him? Why was he alone? Where was his back-up? Why? Why?*

Slowly and reluctantly, officers gradually left the office—some headed home, and some to the parking lot to sit in their cars. But a few remained in the office, shoulders slumped and heads bowed. I was the rookie in the room and alone.

I went up to the barracks and sat on my bed. I never wanted a drink so desperately in my life, but it was against regulations to have liquor in the barracks, so I just sat there. I took out my revolver, unloaded the policy-driven five rounds, then loaded a full six into the cylinder.

# CHAPTER NINE

I sat alone on my cot for more than an hour, polishing my boots, brushing my hat and uniform, and repeatedly loading and unloading my weapon. What was the sense in all of this? I knew that there were dangers in the job, but why did it have to happen to Donny? And so pointless! It wasn't like he was in a shootout with a madman or trying to take down a gang of bank robbers. He was handling the complaint of a couple of drunks fighting!

My mind kept replaying the previous evening and returning to the last chat I had with my partner. We had stopped for a coffee toward the end of our shift—probably around eleven-thirty p.m. The topics were light, and I remembered discussing the upcoming football championship the following Saturday. Donny was disappointed that his team hadn't made the big game. I kidded him about that and how I was, at heart, a Saskatchewan fan. Having taken my recent training in Regina, it seemed natural to carry my support for the Roughriders through the rest of the season. Our parting words were, "See you back at the office." He was my partner, and I would never see him again.

I was sitting there playing *what-ifs* in my mind when the door to the barracks swung open. In walked the staff sergeant with two cases of beer and a bottle of whiskey. With him were a couple of members who had been out on the street earlier. While it was in defiance of policy, this was a different set of circumstances. They pulled chairs from other areas, formed a loose circle near my bed, and broke open the booze. Each took a beer from the case and passed one to me. We leaned in toward one another, lifted our bottles, and clinked them together. "To Donny" was the toast, and we drank.

That was the taste I so desperately wanted.

As the case emptied and the whiskey bottle passed around, tongues loosened, and the officers told stories. About Donny. His character, jokes, moral courage, compassion, and love for the job he did. But there was also anger. At the call-load required of the members, some directed at the force itself and the court system. But much of the anger focussed on the man who killed Cst. Pearson. "He shouldn't have been taken alive." "There should have been some 'street justice' done when they caught him." Statements that would usually not be said aloud. The alcohol and the safety of the group allowed thoughts to be shared.

Over the day, other members came to the room. All carried a bottle or a case of beer. Some left to go home, some crashed on a nearby bed, but the majority stayed on to talk about the previous night. No psychologists or social workers. No counselors or peer-support workers. Just guys who had lost a great friend and a wonderful co-worker.

There was plenty of alcohol to dull the pain and draw the team together. Several times I brought up that I should have been with my partner. I should have gone with him to the call. Maybe if I had been there, he would still be alive.

The staff sergeant pulled his chair over and put his hand on my shoulder. He was still in uniform, and the stars on his sleeve showed his over thirty years of service. "It's not your fault. You were sent to a separate call and did it. The dispatcher decided to send your partner on that call alone—it was a 'nothing call'—just some drunks. We do dozens of these calls a month, so this was not something new or unexpected. But shit happens sometimes."

He paused for a moment. "What do you think the other members are assuming? That it was your mistake? What about the dispatcher believing he should have sent more members? Or the other cars out on the street that heard the call. Should they have gone? There's plenty of guilt and regret to go around. And, regardless of our feelings, nothing is going to change. You'll just have to deal with it in your way." With that, he stood and left the group.

By mid-afternoon, everyone had vacated the barracks, and I was alone. Members on the street and those who had made the arrest took a couple of days off. They needed to recuperate and deal with the tragedy in whatever way they could. Still being under the legal drinking age, I called a bootlegger. I drove to his house, scraping together the little cash I had, and bought four bottles of whiskey to keep in my footlocker. I was going to need them.

The next week was hell. First, there was a debriefing. There, the Inquiry Board analyzed every aspect of the shooting. What went right or wrong? What should we do differently?

An older, streetwise cop asked the question on all our minds. "Are we now going to go to two-man cars or continue having these killings?" The answer was a purely political response. "We'll be looking at that in the days to come. However," the commander added, "from now on, you will always wear your service revolver while in uniform. That policy is in effect as of today." At least there was one thing that was changed.

The sergeant-major arranged for a regimental funeral, but I couldn't go. I was put back on patrol. I never got the chance to say my farewell.

In mid-December, I turned twenty years old.

Sleep became increasingly difficult as my mind would spin with images and scenes that rose unbidden each time I closed my eyes. If I were on dayshift, I would drink each evening heavily until I passed out. I was keeping the demons away. Then I began to drink in the morning to will myself through the day. Spearmint gum, Sen-Sen breath freshener, and Crest toothpaste became my buddies. As best I could, I kept isolated from other members. I grew to be a "problem child" in the RCMP.

So that I could avoid the difficulty of sleep, I volunteered for night shifts. When I did finally fall asleep from sheer exhaustion, nightmares would jar me awake. At times I would shiver and shake so violently I was unable to stand. Other times my muscles would refuse to move, and my eyes would see terrifying images. Later, I learned that these phenomena were not unusual in trauma situations, but to me, as a rookie, they were horrifying. I took increasing risks. I needed to be a one-person car—maybe to prove something to myself or be a "one man against the world."

Because of my willingness to work alone and take any call, I found myself in situations from which I never knew if I would emerge alive. I would go into biker parties and break them up. A prisoner escaping into the bush became a personal challenge. I looked for cars that would try to outrun me and engaged in high-speed pursuits until one of us crashed.

During the next two years, I transferred to several different detachments. I was single, available for duty, and could pack all my stuff in the backseat of my Chevy. Part of it, I believe, was my willingness to work alone and handle calls. Still, I also think that a large portion of the transfers resulted from my being difficult. That, coupled with my drinking and superiors' reluctance to address my chaotic actions, meant they transferred me often.

Throughout that time, I wrecked three patrol cars—two from rolling over in ditches and one from ramming into a car that refused to stop. I became exceptionally good at filling out reports and justifying my aberrant behavior. I loved the thrill of the chase, the adrenaline rush from the speed and danger, and the satisfaction of "winning" against a bad guy. I internalized the belief that there was only one boss out there, and it was me.

I loved to fight. The bigger the guy, the more challenging the task, the more I fought. I lost more scraps than I won, but I sought them out. If I won, I felt like a champ. If I lost, I'd wait a week and try again. I never laid charges. They became a measure of who I was.

I became an angry drunk—with a badge.

# CHAPTER TEN

I had turned twenty-one and could legally get a drink. There were no community bars or lounges where I lived, just sprawling "beer parlors" attached to hotels. It seems odd today, but back then, there was a separate entrance for men and another for "Ladies and Escorts." The tables were two feet in diameter, and the glasses had small lines about a half-inch from the top. It was the fill-line that the bartender had to target as he topped up the glass.

Beer was twenty-five cents a glass, and you could have four glasses on your table at one time. So, a couple of dollars bought you a reasonably good evening. I always used the men's entrance—I had no escort. And, since you were forbidden to drink in a commercial establishment within the bounds of your detachment area, there were many evenings when I drove home and didn't recall ever getting in the car.

Each rural detachment had a small barracks as part of the structure—the same layout as the multi-officer one at Grierson but with only one or two beds. And there was a book on the front desk of the office where you signed out if you were leaving the area, giving your destination and expected time of return. You were the property of the RCMP, and they always wanted to know where you were. I would provide a "general" destination when signing out, but not enough detail for the person in charge to know precisely where I was. I was often too tired and too drunk to sign back in, hoping to complete the appropriate line when I woke up in the morning.

Just before Christmas, I had gone to a party some distance away from my posting. I had a wonderful time. I was the life of the party (in my opinion) and had, in my usual manner, tossed down more whiskey than I should have. I managed to weave my way back to the detachment, completely ignoring the sign-in book. I intended to get up early and fill in the spot with the time I returned. But I didn't wake up in time.

"MacInnes!" The sergeant's voice woke me from my restless and inebriated sleep. "You didn't sign back in, you're pissed, and you're late for your shift. See me in my office immediately."

He was a bit of a hard-ass, and I knew that I wouldn't get off lightly this time. I showered, dressed, and walked down the hall into the office.

"Any excuses?" he asked as I stood in front of him.

I started to explain my lapse, but he held up his hand to silence me.

"This is the third time this month that you've neglected to sign back in and the second time you've been late for duty. You are not going to do this anymore." He took a deep breath and continued.

"You've gotten away with a lot up till now, but your behavior is unacceptable. It will stop right now." I opened my mouth to reply, but he waved me to stop.

"You're a good man and possibly have the makings of a good cop, but you're killing yourself, and I can't let that continue. So, effective immediately and for the next month, you are confined to this detachment area. Except to eat and to go on your patrols, you will not leave the building! Is that clear?" I nodded.

"And I am recommending the commanding officer fine you a hundred dollars, to be deducted from your pay. He will notify the finance people to arrange the money be taken from your salary and put into the fine-fund."

The *fine-fund* was an account accumulated over the year through penalties paid by members who received disciplinary hearings and been levied punishment by their division commander. At Christmas each year, it would be divided amongst the members as a "bonus." A hundred dollars was an enormous amount to someone making the lowest wage of any police in Canada. But there was no appeal. I would have to accept that I was going to be a significant contributor this year. I sure wouldn't get a bonus.

Knowing that the next step would be a dishonorable discharge, I determined to straighten up. And I tried. But working straight through Christmas Eve, Christmas Day, Boxing Day, New Year's Eve, and New Year's Day without having a drink was something I didn't have the strength to do. So, on my next patrol, I called the bootlegger. He agreed to meet me at the edge of the detachment area with a couple of bottles. I was in a marked police car. It was awkward. Here he was selling illegal liquor and should have been arrested. Here I was, buying illegal whiskey—in uniform. But he had become used to me over the years, and when I explained my dilemma, he agreed and brought the bottles. Over the month of being confined to barracks, we met another four times. Smuggling them into my quarters wasn't much of a challenge, and, as before, I hid them in my footlocker. But I survived.

A few members who knew me and the self-sabotage actions I seemed to take regularly wondered why I just didn't quit being a cop. But I liked the job—the uncertainty of each call, the sense there was a yet-undefined purpose for me, and especially the adrenaline surges from taking risks. But I also knew that I was putting myself in increasing jeopardy with each dodgy decision I made. It was becoming a habit—maybe even an addiction. Coupled with the booze, I couldn't see a good ending. And, perhaps, my commanders saw the same thing.

By late spring, the "brass" transferred me to a temporary position at a one-man detachment in a national park. My job was enforcing the law, patrolling the area, assisting tourists with inquiries or problems, and being back-up to the park wardens. The organization had set aside a small cabin for my use. It consisted of an office that doubled as a kitchen, living room, and dining area. A tiny bedroom and bathroom/shower area completed the layout. I was on my own. I'd try to get my life back on track.

It was an enjoyable summer. I met visitors from all parts of the world. A young couple from Australia driving a modified van stayed a week, camping in a small clearing just below my cabin. In the evening, I would drop over, have a coffee, and visit. They had been on the road for over a year, stopping at various points across North America and exploring the nearby towns and areas of historical interest. Two single men on motorcycles stayed for a couple of days, and I got to know them. The father of one of the bikers was an officer in New York City, and the second one had been accepted into the state police and would be starting his training in the fall.

They were intrigued to learn about RCMP officers' training and deployment. I shared the joys of working in rural settings and Canada's law and court systems, which were quite different from our American cousins'. I did not, however, share the dark side of policing. That was personal.

By mid-summer, I was increasingly comfortable in my new role, enjoying the park's quietness, the unique aspects of living alone, and doing my cooking and cleaning. I got a German Shepherd dog to keep me company, and the hours spent walking the bush and training him in tracking, and searching was one highlight of my summer. I say *one* as, late on a sunny August afternoon, another highlight was coming out of a camping area.

As was our usual practice, I would team up several times a week with a park warden to do a patrol of the park. This time we were in his truck rather than in my marked police car. The wardens had just received authorization to place red lights on the roofs of their vehicles, and my driver was anxious to try it out. The powder-blue '66 Mustang, coming out onto the road ahead of us, seemed an excellent opportunity. As the vehicle turned in front of us, we glimpsed the driver—a young woman with shoulder-length blond hair, sunglasses, and a T-shirt.

Joe, driving with one hand on the wheel, reached for the switch. "I'm going to stop her," he said, turning on the roof light.

I looked over. "Why? She's just coming out of the tenting area; she made a full stop at the sign. What reason do you have to stop her?"

He just grinned. "I think you need a date."

"No. I don't need a date!" I was not a great social person, and the thought of asking a stranger that we had stopped on the road for a date was entirely outside my comfort zone. Besides, what was I going to say was the reason we stopped her?

"I'll go up and check her out," Joe declared as he pulled the truck close in behind her moving car. The driver didn't stop.

"I hope this doesn't end up in a chase," I murmured. A young woman, alone in her car, and we were trying to stop her for absolutely no reason at all. Except maybe that Joe thought I needed a date. I thought this whole thing would end up as one of those "confined to barracks" type incidents.

Joe was right on her tail as we wound our way through the park. As this was the first time he had used the new equipment in a "real" situation, he didn't realize that due to the truck's height and how close he was to the Mustang, the driver couldn't see his flashing red lights. It was a mile or two before he realized his error and dropped back a few vehicle lengths. She stopped immediately.

"I'll tell her she was speeding and get her driver's license and name," he said, opening the door.

"No!" I exclaimed. "She'll know you're lying. She wasn't speeding!"

"Then, I'll just tell her that her car looked suspicious." With that, he closed the door and walked up to the driver's window. I cringed.

# CHAPTER ELEVEN

Joe was a great guy, and over the summer, I got to know him well. He was about ten years older than me and had been with the National Park Service for half a decade. We would patrol together a couple of times a week. If we were in my vehicle, our focus would be on the roadways and checking on the cabins, concession stands, and camping areas surrounding the lake. If we used his truck, we would drive the back trails, ensuring the small herd of buffalo was doing well, the beaver dams weren't starting to flood the roads, or, sometimes, just chatting with guests checking in at the visitors' center. Stopping a vehicle leaving the campground was unusual, and I could only sit in the truck, highly embarrassed.

The young woman in the Mustang rolled down her window as Joe approached. They spoke for several minutes, and I saw her pass over some documents to him. I assumed it was her driver's license and vehicle registration. He pointed toward me, and the lady stuck her head out the window and looked in my direction. He waved me to come up to the car. Reluctantly I got out of the truck and joined them.

Joe took my shoulder and moved me closer to the open window. "I'd like to introduce you to Dee," he said, presenting his free hand toward the young lady. "She's from the area, is single, and isn't a camper here in the park. She's a lifeguard at the youth camp down by the lake."

"And Dee," he said with a bit of a grin. "This is Constable MacInnes; he's the Mountie assigned to the park for the summer. I think the two of you should get together." With that, he headed back to the truck, leaving me with only two choices—say "hi" and go back with Joe or try to salvage a bit of my dignity and see if I could advance this brief introduction.

Knowing I was about to breach several policies, I pulled out my notebook and pen. I covered my nervousness with a cloak of officialness and asked, "Could I have your name, phone number, and address?" I immediately felt like a fool as I held her driver's license in my hand that contained her full name—Derenda Algie—date of birth, and residence. But she provided them again, including her home phone number. I tucked the pad back in my pocket and returned to the truck.

"So, how did it go? Did you get her phone number?"

I nodded.

"Isn't she gorgeous? I mean, long blond hair, great figure—and drives a Mustang! What more could you want?"

"I don't know," I replied. "She's way out of my class."

"Bullshit. You're a Mountie, for God's sake! And single. Give her a call. Maybe she'll say yes. What can it hurt?"

We hadn't moved from the side of the road. The red lights flashed as the Mustang pulled away. I just wanted to get out of there. It was getting awkward.

"Maybe I will. Can we just leave now?" Joe pulled back onto the roadway, did a U-turn, and we headed back to the main beach area and the concession booth to grab a coffee before returning to our tasks. He couldn't shut up about the girl in the Mustang.

Later that evening, sitting alone in my tiny cabin, my thoughts returned to the encounter on the road. *What if I do phone? What's the worst that can happen? What if she says, "No, I don't want to go on a date? What if she says, 'yes, I'd like to go on a date?' What if she gets to know me for who I am and then dumps me?* Do I take the chance?

It was after midnight when my mind settled on the answer. Yes, I would take the chance and give her a call. I headed for bed. For the first time in almost two years, I didn't need a drink to put me to sleep.

The following afternoon I decided to head to town, pick up some supplies, and fill up my tank at the gas station. As I signed the chit that would bill the RCMP for my gas, I saw a phone booth against the wall. I dug out my notebook and looked at the last entry: her name, address, and phone number.

I pulled a handful of change from my pockets. I'd make the call.

I dropped a dime into the slot and dialed the number. "Hello," came the response as a woman answered the call. "Hello," I said in reply. "Hello, hello, hello," the woman said before hanging up. I tried it again.

Like the previous attempt, I inserted the dime, dialed, and got the same response from the same woman. "Hello." Then a pause as I tried to make the connection. After several more "hellos," I could hear the woman say to someone at that end, "I think it's some crackpot," then she hung up.

Discouraged, I returned to my car. After reflecting on the experience for a couple of minutes, I decided to give it one more try. Entering the small booth, I finally had the sense to read the information on the phone booth's side. *Dial the number first and, when answered, insert 10 cents to complete the call.* I had royally screwed up. I had been putting money in the payphone before I dialed the number! What a dumbass. I dialed one last time.

"Hello." This time, someone else answered the phone. I slipped the coin into the slot.

"Hi, is Dee there?"

"This is Dee," came the reply. *Now, what do I say?*

"Umm, this is Ross. You probably don't remember, but I'm the Mountie that stopped you yesterday in the park." *What a stupid thing to say! That SHE couldn't remember being stopped by a cop less than twenty-four hours ago?*

"Of course, I remember. You were with the warden that told me I was driving a suspicious car."

"Ah, yes. I was with the warden. And you were driving that blue Mustang." *As if she wouldn't remember which car she was driving.* I stumbled right to the point.

"I was wondering if you'd like to go out with me tomorrow night?" There was no response. *Maybe we got disconnected?* I repeated my question.

"Hello. Would you like to go out tomorrow night?"

"Sure, we can go out. What time will you pick me up?" I was elated. She said *yes*!

"I'll pick you up at seven p.m.," I replied. "I have your address—I copied it off your driver's license." *Now I was feeling like a stalker!*

"Sounds good. I'll see you at seven tomorrow then."

I can't fully remember the intervening twenty-four hours, only that I was nervous, excited, elated, scared, and worried. I was way out of my depth. Here was a beautiful, sophisticated "city girl," and I was a country boy from back-ass Manitoba, a slow learner, ADHD, and felt dumber than a horseshoe. But she had agreed to go out with me!

I pulled up in front of her house at the agreed-upon time and knocked. Her mother met me at the door. She was smiling, but I could tell she was very suspicious of this guy who was taking her only daughter on a date very awkwardly and maybe even inappropriately.

Dee moved up beside her mother. "Hi, Ross, I'm just about ready. I'll be with you in a minute." I didn't know what she still had to do. To me, she was perfect. Her hair had been done; her makeup applied, her blue dress shimmied into—she was beautiful. I had no idea where we would go or what we would be doing. I had dressed in my usual—blue jeans, a long-sleeve shirt, and cowboy boots. Quite a contrast. I felt like a hillbilly on his first trip to town.

She came back to the door and out onto the step. In the evening light, she looked even more stunning. Walking to the car, she turned and asked, "Where are we going?"

"I thought we'd go to a drive-in movie," I replied. Dee stopped in the middle of the sidewalk.

She didn't say anything, but I could almost hear her thoughts. *A drive-in? On a first date? With a guy I'd only met once on the side of a road? When I spent all that time doing my makeup, fixing my hair, and picking out a dress?*

"Sounds good," she answered as I opened the car door. She settled in the seat, and I went around and climbed behind the wheel.

It wasn't the usual first date. I hadn't brought flowers or chocolates, hadn't appropriately dressed, had no idea where we would go, and had my German Shepherd in the back seat. I spilled coffee on her dress, couldn't carry a conversation properly, and pinched her fingers in the door. But I wanted to see her again.

When I walked her up to her door later that night, I nervously asked, "Would you like to go out again?"

"Yes, I would. I had a great time." I was elated.

The next weekend I took her shooting. We spent the day plinking at targets in an old gravel pit. She fired my .22 and my ancient .303 Lee-Enfield rifle. She even fired my service revolver. I thought: *This is someone with whom I could spend my life.*

Our second date turned into a third, then a fourth and fifth. Within three months, I popped the question. This time I made sure the date was proper. I brought my date a dozen red roses, reserved a table at a high-end restaurant, and booked tickets to the live Reveen show. I had bought a ring and asked Dee to marry me.

# CHAPTER TWELVE

Back in the day, the process of getting married in the RCMP was not easy. First, you had to apply to the commissioner for permission to marry. Headquarters sent out for you to list the names and addresses of the prospective bride's family. Parents, siblings, grandparents, aunts, and uncles. Second, you had to prepare a financial report listing all your assets and liabilities and submit the various forms to the commissioner. They investigated your future relatives (in case any were communists, criminals, or low moral character). They also had to decide if the bride would be "appropriate" for a member of the force and if you had the financial stability to support the marriage and a possible future family.

Once the commissioner "approved" the bride, you had a second set of forms to complete. To be married in uniform (a regimental wedding), you had to list all the components that might require you to wear the Red Serge uniform. The groomsmen, Honor Guard, and even the ushers were all RCMP members and needed permission. Once approved, you needed a third level of clearance—this time to use the lances as part of the Honor Guard. Finally, with all requests approved by the various authorities, we finalized our plans. It was less than eight months from the moment I met her on the highway when we said, "I do."

Our wedding took place in a small church in Fort Saskatchewan, Alberta. The sight of a full regimental wedding in the town caused curiosity and comment by the locals. As well as me, the groomsmen dressed in Walking Out Order. It consisted of a Stetson hat, red serge, blue trousers (straight leg instead of the flared breeches), congress boots with box spurs, and brown gloves. We did not wear our revolver or holster, nor did we sport the handcuff or ammo pouch. In Mountie terms, it was called a "stripped Sam Browne." Ushers and the Honor Guard members wore the more traditional Review Order that substituted breeches for the straight-leg trousers. They also wore sidearm, ammo, and handcuff pouches on full Sam Browne.

The evening before the "big day," I polished leather, brushed my tunic and trousers, and ensured that my old Chevy was as clean and sparkling as possible. My parents and younger brother had driven out from Manitoba to be a part of the big day, and my older brother, also a member of the RCMP, had agreed to be my best man. Dee's father had died from a heart attack about four years earlier, so her favorite uncle from Toronto had flown out to walk her down the aisle. He was an imposing figure. Over 6'3", with iron-grey hair and a rigid stance, he presented as if he were the event's commanding officer.

With our families and guests decked out in their finest, the minister in a long black robe, and with my brother and fellow officers beside me, we awaited the bride. After what seemed to be an excessive amount of time, there she was! The girl who was to become my wife came down the aisle on the arm of her Uncle Jim. What a rush of emotion! With Dee's mother and extended family seated to the left and my parents and family sitting to the right, the minister addressed the assembled group. "Who gives this woman to be married?" Dee's uncle, in a deep baritone matching his height and bearing, responded. "Her mother and I do." He then took Dee's right hand and placed it in mine.

Caught up in the wonder of the moment, I could only respond with the "I do's" when prompted by the officiating minister. But it was not without worry that I stood there at rigid attention. Turning to face the bride and then turning back to the minister to reply to his questions, I had accidentally crossed my spurs with the shuffling of positions. Tangling parts of my uniform was not an unusual occurrence for me, as I regularly got my spurs snarled, but I had always been able to subtly move my feet to figure out which foot was free. But this time, I had no idea which was atop the other. It must have been amusing to the guests to see me shuffling my feet back and forth. I lifted one heel then the other as the service wound down to the "I now pronounce you man and wife."

Maybe they thought I had to take a pee?

As we turned to make our way to the registry book, I had to guess what foot was atop the other. I leaned forward and stepped off with my right leg. I had decided that this was the foot that was the top spur—big mistake. My right leg refused to move. The forward lean and balance point was way off. It was my *left* spur that was on top. I stumbled. In a crude attempt to keep from hitting the carpet-covered floor and ruining the day, I wildly grabbed anything within reach. The church platform was small, and there were not many options: the flower stand, the preacher, the podium, or the baptismal font. I grabbed my new wife. Perhaps it was a sign of what would come throughout our lives—holding on to Dee to keep from falling on my face.

The reception was "dry." We did not serve wine, and there was no bar. My parents were teetotallers, and we wanted to honor their faith. Besides, I was familiar with cops and their "any party is a good party" philosophy. Later I learned they had their get-together, and I heard it was a good one.

Members of the force were notorious for setting up elaborate pranks on newly married couples. Often, if they had the vehicle's license number that would head out on the honeymoon, they would circulate a "stolen car" hot sheet. Or they might place a note in the gas-tank filler lid, indicating that the woman in the car was a hostage and needed rescue. We had hidden our get-away car in a downtown parkade for just that possibility. We got away clean and out of our sub-division without incident.

Upon returning from our honeymoon in California, we settled in our new detachment. My summer posting at the national park had come to an end, and I transferred for the fifth time in two years, this time to a detachment with a more extensive complement of officers and an attached Highway Patrol section covering the area's main roadways. It was a busy posting, with summer resorts, rural farmlands, a scattering of small towns, and several First Nations' reservations (in that era referred to as Indians). General detachment patrol duties were routine: answering calls, checking businesses for break-ins on the night shift, marching in local parades, and ensuring the teenagers parked along lonely roads weren't drinking beer.

★ ★ ★

The RCMP is a federal department responsible for enforcing laws and regulations common to all provinces and territories. In addition to their national mandate, they are often "contracted" to provide policing services to cities, towns, and municipal districts. Several eastern regions have provincial police agencies, and most cities have elected to maintain their individual policing services. However, the RCMP has agreements with most provinces and provides contract services to several cities (particularly in British Columbia) and most municipal districts throughout Western Canada.

Historically, First Nations people were governed by the British Crown through Queen's representatives. After Confederation in 1867, that responsibility fell to the various provinces and territories. The Indian Act was passed in 1876 by the Government of Canada. Enforcement related to the legislation fell to the RCMP. The Act defined who was considered an "Indian," rules around land ownership, rights of men versus women, on-reserve members, non-treaty Indians, Metis, and a host of other regulatory issues.

Of significance was the entire subject of intoxicants. Regulations around the drinking, selling, trading, making, or possession of liquor were the basis of many of the Act's decrees. It was, therefore, a significant part of our detachment duties.

As the agency responsible for law enforcement, we conducted general patrols on the roads and trails throughout the various reserves. And we responded to calls for assistance several times per week. The administration of law on the various reserves is often related to alcohol issues. Calls for help in family disputes or fights between individuals who felt other community members had wronged them were commonplace.

Historically, politicians had passed the Indian Act through Parliament to control and assimilate Indigenous peoples and their communities. The various treaties agreed upon throughout Canada's history differentiated in a significant way: the conducting of the lives of Indians compared to the lives of other Canadians. Through legislative amendments over the years, even specific dances and celebrations were deemed "illegal" and outlawed.

Initially, the RCMP had critical roles as protectors and partners in developing reserves and attending to the Indigenous people's welfare. Increasingly, however, they were being viewed as adversaries and agents of control.

And while the laws and regulations were drafted and formed in far-away Ottawa by politicians and bureaucrats, it was left up to the local RCMP constable to enforce those regulations. Unable to avoid those responsibilities, many force members developed apathy and cynicism toward both the Indigenous populations and the government that formed the regulatory conditions they were to enforce.

How in God's name was a white farm kid from Manitoba to know the difference between a Round Dance, a Buffalo Dance, or a Sun Dance? And the songs? With absolutely no knowledge of the native language, we could not know which songs were deemed illegal and which were OK. It was confusing, frustrating, and, ultimately, a moral injustice.

# CHAPTER THIRTEEN

Depot's training covered dozens of federal acts; however, there was little training or background to the Indian Act or its later amendments. As part of the force's history, we studied the North-West (Riel) Rebellion, the Battle of Batoche, and the Provisional Government of Saskatchewan (which included parts of Manitoba, Saskatchewan, and Alberta). Metis and First Nations peoples fought these battles against the Government of Canada. The Federal forces were much better equipped and had far more resources at their disposal. As a result, the Riel rebellion failed. After a short trial, the leader, Louis Riel, was hanged, and his top commander escaped to Montana. But the demands for equality and justice from the Indigenous and Metis communities did not stop. It just simmered beneath the surface, and from time to time, even today, it surfaces.

Although Parliament had amended the Indian Act the year before the rebellion, the Riel-led forces' defeat impelled a rapid expansion of the residential school policy. Its purpose was to eliminate Indigenous language and culture and replace them with English and Christian beliefs. The Act made attendance at day school, residential schools, or industrial schools mandatory for children between six and fifteen. As one politician said, "to kill the Indian in the child."

The Indian residential school system was funded by the Canadian government and administered by Christian churches. As many Indigenous communities were in remote areas, the children were placed not in a local day-school but a residential school.

The contracted churches built the schools and residential structures in locations to make family visits almost impossible. It was the policy of Hayter Reed, the commissioner of Indian Affairs, during the late 1800s. The result was that this "removal" robbed the children of their native language and culture and subjected many to horrendous abuse and even death. Apprehending and removing the child from the reserve to the residential school fell on the school's administrators. However, the local RCMP were frequently called upon to assist.

As police officers, we would often meet during the shift to debrief one another, share stories, or, sometimes, bitch about things that were going on. A common topic was the enforcement of the Indian Act and all its various clauses and sub-sections. While disliking the overall Act, members most detested compelling families to release their child to the residential school system.

Although it was supposed to be "by permission," the economic incentives were significant. The government provided funds on a per-student basis; thus, the bulk of the school's income came through the number of children enrolled. Should parents refuse to send their children, the government imposed a financial penalty. It was always a win for the church schools, a loss for the families—loss of a child or loss of income.

Members would share stories of parents attacking them as school administrators apprehended their sons or daughters. The sworn officers found themselves in a position of supporting and protecting something they felt was inherently wrong. Those assigned to be a part of the apprehension would actively avoid a subsequent assignment. For the police, it was a lose-lose situation. They would lose their connection with members of the reserve, and in the process, part of their souls.

★ ★ ★

I was working on some reports at my desk when two men and a woman came into the detachment. They appeared dressed for business—the men in suits and ties, the woman in a dress. Through the window behind them, I could see the front end of a blue passenger van. They stood quietly at the counter, waiting. I was about to go forward and greet them; however, another member already headed their way.

They presented documents, and the member spoke to them. After examining the papers, he called for the corporal to come to the front. After a brief conversation, the corporal waved me over.

I left my desk and joined the group at the counter. "These folks are from the mission school for the Indians," he said as I stood beside him. "I guess a couple of kids didn't show up, or maybe they just didn't want to go back to the school, so they're here to go pick them up."

I nodded. I knew from the comments made over the past few months that the officers did not like to do these calls. I glanced around and realized that the other constables had left the office and disappeared.

The corporal pushed the papers along the desk for me to read. I picked them up.

"There are the names and the location where these folks believe the family is living," he said, looking at me but pointing at the three people across the counter. "Your job isn't to apprehend the kids, but you're going along just to make sure everything goes safely."

I nodded. "OK, I'll grab my hat." I looked at the three and said, "I'll go with you."

"No. I want you to take the patrol car and follow them to the place. And after they leave with the kids, you can take a quick loop through the reserve." I nodded my understanding of the corporal's comment.

I grabbed my hat and briefcase, the keys off the hook, and headed for my car.

I followed their van on the thirty-minute drive to the reserve. They seemed to know where they were going, although we did take a couple of wrong turns. It was just after lunch when we arrived at the home where they believed the children were.

The house was typical of many on the reserve: a small, beige bungalow with dilapidated front steps; several older-model cars in the yard; a bicycle lying on its side; some toys scattered around. There was no fence indicating the property line or any significant landscaping—just a couple of sickly trees growing near one of the cars.

As we approached, I saw the door close and a face peering out from one of the windows. There seemed little doubt that they knew who we were and why we were there.

The three church representatives left their car and walked to the front door. The top landing was small, so only one of the men mounted the stair and knocked. There was no response.

"I saw one of the kids looking out the window, so we know they're in there," the woman said as she put one foot on the lower step.

"That's good enough," the man at the top of the step said as he turned the knob and opened the door. The second man, then the woman, entered behind him. Briefly, I stood at the entrance, then one of the men motioned me forward. I entered and looked around.

Sparsely furnished, the central area contained a couple of old couches, two plastic lawn chairs, and a low table covered in toys—no TV or stereo. A couple of framed pictures and a calendar completed the decorations.

A walk through the kitchen area showed open shelves with a few cans of food, some cups, plates, bowls, and, on the counter, a small plastic tub with cutlery. Below the lower shelf hung some meat drying.

There was a sink piled high with dishes and a pail of water standing beside the sink. But there was no running water.

"This is disgusting," the church-lady muttered as she passed me to head down the hall.

It wasn't disgusting to me. It felt kind of familiar. The house and furnishings were not significantly dissimilar to the home where I grew up. We even had an outhouse tucked into the bush. It stunk in the summer, but we controlled that with powdered lime. The Manitoba winters of minus-forty and driving snowstorms were a different story.

"Here they are!" one of the men called back to his companions as he opened the door to one of the two bedrooms. I moved forward and looked over his shoulder.

Sitting on the bed holding a baby, was a young woman who looked to be in her mid-twenties. Two young boys sat beside her—one on each side. Hanging onto her leg was another child who appeared to be about two or three.

The baby was crying, and the young woman rocked the infant back and forth, trying her best to soothe them. The older boys looked at us with fear and struggled to find space as close to their mother as they could. The toddler had buried his face against her leg.

Three stern-looking adults dressed in city clothes and a Mountie in uniform crowded into the doorway of the tiny room. It must have been terrifying.

"We're here to take the two boys to school." The well-dressed woman moved into the room and knelt to be at eye-level with the mother.

The young woman looked at her two sons beside her. "I talked to the chief, and he said we don't have to send them to the residential school." She had tears in her eyes.

"And he's right," the taller man in the doorway replied. "You don't have to send your kids to school. But you do know that if you don't, your family allowance cheque gets cut off, don't you?"

She nodded and softly said through her tears, "But why don't we have a school here on the reserve so our kids can come home every day?"

The man quickly answered. "That's not our decision. We have no authority over where the government puts schools. All we can provide is the one we have."

"And," the man continued, "you can visit the kids any time you want. All you need is to get a visiting permit from the Indian agent."

The second man pushed his way into the room. "So, what's it going to be? Are you going to keep the kids at home and lose the family allowance? Or let them go to the school where they will get a great education, live with other kids their age, get great food and exercise, and be able to come back later and help you with the younger kids?"

The intimidation factor of four white authority-figures in that small house must have been overwhelming. The young mother, still sitting on the bed, continued to sob.

"I'll tell you what," the churchwoman said, putting her hand on the young mother's knee. "Let's give the boys a chance to see the school for a week. If they don't like it, they can come back home. How about that?"

I knew that was a lie. The school officials knew it was a lie. And, I believe, the young mother also knew it was a lie. But what were the alternatives?

Settling the baby in her lap, she wrapped her arms around her two young sons and nodded her acceptance.

With that nod, the two men moved forward, each taking a boy by the hand and leading them from the house to the waiting van. My role as a police officer was not to participate in the apprehension but to ensure there was no fighting. But violence begins in the heart—not the hand.

I returned to the detachment, put the car away, and booked off my shift. Something was wrong here. It might have been legal, but it wasn't moral.

I later learned that a social worker had gone to the house, apprehended the two remaining children, and placed them in foster care.

I cannot imagine what impact losing all four children in the span of a few weeks had on that young mother. In later years this, and similar actions were taken across the country and became known as the "Sixties Scoop."

The long-term effect of this system, still with us today, is a greater frequency of trauma-related actions such as alcoholism, drug abuse, family violence, and suicide amongst Indigenous communities.

My nightmares returned. I could not do this anymore.

# CHAPTER FOURTEEN

There were plenty of calls to respond to, a vast area to patrol, and the ever-present files to complete. But the incidents of child apprehension on the reserve never left my mind. I was angry, I was frustrated, and, yes, I was ashamed of the role I had played.

I would attempt to raise the issue with other force members, but they would either change the subject quickly or pass it off as "it's just part of the job." It was something you didn't discuss. But I could also sense *their* frustration, anger, and shame over being put in situations against their moral code.

I recalled a time from my childhood where we were snowed in during a particularly vicious storm and had little food for two weeks—only buckwheat as nourishment. Buckwheat pancakes, buckwheat porridge, buckwheat soup—then repeat each day until the plows came, and we could get to town. What if a neighbor reported my parents and the four boys taken from them for being "neglected"?

Due to our small house's limited space, my two older brothers had to sleep on the floor. The mattress stood against the wall during the day, then plopped down at night, and the two dropped off to sleep. Was that neglect or abuse? It wasn't camping—it was a way of life.

Raised in a loving home, all four of us went on to successful careers, stable, loving marriages, and great kids. Why was our situation different from those on the reserves? What would we have become if the government had subjected us to that same law?

★ ★ ★

There was something I didn't recognize at the time. The cumulative effects of the murder of my partner, the daily stressors of policing, and now, the emotional drain of enforcing the Indian Act were having a severe impact on me.

I was on edge much of the time. I became withdrawn and moody, and my health deteriorated. I couldn't fall asleep quickly, and when I did, nightmares filled the darkness. I didn't share any of this with anyone. I was afraid that other members would view me as weak, not strong enough to be a cop. I tried to "just get over it."

When I'd submitted the "request to marry," we'd understood that wives of mounted police officers were considered *supernumerary members* of the force. That meant that, if needed, the individual in charge of the detachment could call upon the wives to assist in detachment duties. And the RCMP would not pay them for their service. We also knew that this was the reason for such thorough background checks on the prospective wife.

During our posting to that area, there were several times that the Sergeant called upon Dee to provide "matron service." Should a woman be arrested for any crime more severe than being drunk, one of the member's wives would be called in to do matron duty. There were no female sworn officers in the RCMP in that era, and our wives were called *the second man*.

She was required to search the female prisoner for any weapons, stolen property, drugs, or other prohibited items before placing the individual in the cells. It was a big shock to this young city girl, but she did it with grace and compassion.

On one occasion, the officers had arrested three Aboriginal people for robbery. A woman in her late twenties was a part of the group.

The sergeant phoned Dee and asked her to search the woman and provide "guard duty" overnight. The woman would appear before a magistrate in the morning court session to set bail and release conditions. My wife got a glimpse of the hopelessness and abject poverty that the arrestee displayed as she was searched and put behind bars.

What Dee did not know was that I had met this woman before. She was the young mother who had lost two sons to the residential school and the other two children to foster care services. I had pushed the original incidents to the far reaches of my mind, but this brought it all home once again.

Over the coming weeks, my bride sensed a change in me. While supporting my career, shift work, and the isolation of being a "cop family," she never pressed me to relay what happened. Dee provided time and opportunity to let her inside my silent world, but I could not share my struggles. I was afraid she then would also get the nightmares, guilt, and fears. Like me, she just hung on and prayed for my safety and better times to come.

Things had to change.

★ ★ ★

I arranged to meet with a sergeant that I had gotten to know and with whom I had spoken after Donny's murder. I opened up to him and shared my concerns. While I loved being a part of the RCMP, I felt I could not continue my current role as a constable in my assigned detachment.

The sergeant wasn't a psychologist, social worker, or even a part of the personnel section. He was an old cop who had seen it all and accumulated over twenty-five years of service throughout Canada. And, I trusted his judgment.

After listening to my concerns, he offered three options I could take. The first was to continue where I was and wait until my time was served on the detachment and I got a transfer (usually in three to five years). The second option was to apply to a specialty unit that would allow me to move to another area of work within the police force (such as the Police Service Dog section, Highway Patrol, or a desk assignment in an urban center). The third alternative was to resign and find another occupation.

I immediately rejected the third possibility. I loved being a member of the RCMP. The feeling of being a part of a mission-driven organization, the camaraderie, the interactions with the community, and, yes, I loved the adrenaline that came as part of responding to an unknown situation. With all my heart, I wanted to remain a part of this organization.

As I had always enjoyed working with animals and had a particular affinity with dogs, I applied for the Police Service Dog Section. Within a couple of weeks, I received a memo from the personnel section that I could train as a "quarry" for the dog section. I was to report to the non-commissioned officer in charge (NCO i/c) of the unit and participate in a week-long training refresher course in Jasper, Alberta. I was elated!

The quarry work was acting like an escaped criminal tracked down by a dog-and-handler team and, suitably padded, being the target of attack work. A week of laying tracks through the bush, hiding "stolen" goods, dropping evidence in unusual places, and listening in on theory and case law related to the use of dogs in police work was exhilarating. The openness and acceptance of the senior handlers were very encouraging.

There were six "potential" handlers in our quarries group, and the NCO advised that there would be two selected for the next training class.

I returned to my detachment and awaited the notice. It came.

*Constable MacInnes performed all his duties with attention and dedication. He was competent in all areas, and it is our opinion he will qualify as a Police Service Dog handler in two or three years.*

Two or three years! I tried another approach.

I applied for a transfer to Highway Patrol. Maybe in this way, I could remain in my detachment area but would not have the task of enforcing the Indian Act. It might be a good compromise and give me the time-served needed to become part of the dog section.

Accident investigation, impaired-driving criteria, and pursuit driving were a few of the in-service classes I sought and completed. The most complicated program was the radar course. In those days, the use of radar to monitor and enforce speed violations was in its infancy. Tripods, trunks full of huge batteries, tuning forks, complex formulas, and communication with "catch cars" were part of the curriculum. I passed the exams and received my speed-radar certification.

Once again, I awaited the results of my transfer request. While the summation sent to personnel was complimentary and supportive, it also recommended a two-to-three-year waiting period.

Things certainly weren't going the way I had hoped. While both requests had been positive and complimentary, I knew that I wouldn't be going anywhere for two, maybe three years. I had one more option.

The RCMP is very supportive of educational upgrading. Having not completed high school, I felt that a lateral transfer to an urban center would enable me to develop my education and keep working for an organization I respected. It would also serve to give me the time-in needed to qualify for a specialty unit. I applied for a transfer.

I had submitted three requests to move from my current position, so the personnel section knew I was not content where I was. Reviewing my previous behaviors and conduct, they flatly turned me down. Transfer denied.

During this time frame, I continued to have nightmares. I felt a crushing pressure to do something, *anything*, to get them to stop and for my mind to reach back for something ordinary. It was becoming too much to bear. I couldn't fathom how other members handled the darkness. Although the opportunity was there, I refused to talk to anyone about my fears, worry, and guilt. I became more and more withdrawn and anxious.

I learned of an opportunity to work in the Arctic with a guide and outfitting company. I used that excuse as a rationale for a quick decision.

I quit.

I was no longer a member of the Royal Canadian Mounted Police.

## CHAPTER FIFTEEN

After turning in my revolver, uniform, ID card, and other elements that provided me with a sense of identity as a Mountie, I walked away feeling empty. I had no mission, no purpose, and no value. Where once members would give me a wave, a clap on the shoulder, or share a coffee, now they would not even make eye contact.

It was not like I had left the force, but that I had never even been there. I knew that I had made a mistake in resigning.

The die was cast, and Dee and I decided to move to Yellowknife in the Northwest Territories and Palmer Outfitters' base. Selling the Mustang and my '58 Chevy was a hard decision, but the money was enough to buy an older three-quarter-ton truck and a used 10' X 45' mobile home. The Dodge was sorely underpowered for the trailer's size, but we couldn't turn back now. I had made an irreversible decision. We took the next step in our lives with a mixture of excitement and trepidation.

The truck had been serviced and cleaned up for the trip. An extra forty-five-gallon drum of gasoline chained into the box, and a few tools crammed into an old wooden crate. We loaded the mobile home with our personal effects and raided the shelves at the local grocery store for provisions distributed evenly across the floor.

It was time to go.

We pulled out of Edmonton in the early morning to begin the three-day trip to Yellowknife. We hadn't yet cleared the city limits before realizing the truck's 318 cubic-inch motor was inadequate for the task. And so, we made the thousand-mile trip in third gear and a top speed of forty miles an hour.

The highway into Peace River was under construction, and the hill down to the bridge crossing was wet mud. We slipped and slid down the steep detour and pushed the switch that controlled the trailer brakes. Taking the first side-street we found, we discovered we had turned into a residential subdivision alley under development. It took two hours to work our way out, but who cared?

It poured rain the whole trip. The gravel road was slick, and patches of fog rose above each river and creek. A blown tire on the trailer required a full day's delay. The challenge of maneuvering the rig onto the barge across the Mackenzie River tested my driving skills, and potholes that threatened to destroy axles slowed our journey even more. It may have been a short-lived adventure, but I relished every minute of it.

The federal government had recently designated Yellowknife the Territories' capital, and it was a boomtown in full swing. No place to park the trailer other than in one of the Palmer brothers' driveways, prices sky-high, and folks were arriving every day. The territorial government transferred from Ottawa to the new capital, and Help Wanted posters were in every business's windows. One traffic light, a few stop signs, and just a gravel strip at the airport. The last of the gold rush towns.

We took a couple of days to settle in and become familiar with the town and the immediate area. There was only one road in and, branching off from the center were two gravel roads—one to the Giant Yellowknife Gold Mine just to the north of the town and the other to the Con Gold Mine on the south side. They were the two largest employers in the area and, to no small degree, were the founders of Yellowknife.

Of interest was that each had a baseball team that played weekly games for the community's entertainment. In theory, each player was also a miner but seldom seen in the shafts. Instead, they practiced all week for that one game. But they were the mainstay of show business in the area.

Being claustrophobic, I didn't want to be a miner, and my baseball skills were minimal at best, so I decided to pursue the task of guiding and outfitting with the company that had lured me north. They were a small enterprise with an office/repair shop on an inlet of the Great Slave Lake. It was quite a rundown affair, but there was only space for a dock and a shop with all the town's growth. The Palmer family ran the operation, with Zane as the pilot/mechanic of the ancient single-engine Mark IV Norseman. Similar in size and performance to the single-engine Otter, this old plane was the mainstay of their business.

And Zane was one heck of a bush pilot. I once asked him how many hours he had flown. He simply replied, "I don't know. I threw my logbook away when I hit 10,000 hours twelve years ago."

My first glimpse of his skill was on the second day of our arrival. Zane worked out of Norman Wells on the Mackenzie River, where he contracted to stake some gold-mining claims. He had been operating on skis due to the snow, but now he needed to switch over to pontoons for the upcoming hunting season.

The radio in "the office" came alive as Zane announced his pending arrival. The three remaining family members and I headed outside to see how this landing was going to go. The plane was still on skis, the "home lake" was now ice-free, and the pontoons laid out on the ramp leading into the water. The plane buzzed low, looked at the landing conditions, climbed back up, then readied itself for a landing on the open lake.

Flaps down and nose up, he skimmed low over the houses on the bay and made his approach. The skis touched down, sending a considerable spray out and behind the arriving plane. One could hear the engine alternating between revving up and throttling down as the pilot kept the silver and red craft from nosing into the water and crashing. Like a skipped stone, he headed for the ramp. Still going strong as he closed the distance, Zane killed the engine about fifty feet from shore and, with the skis sinking lower in the water, drifted up onto the ramp beside the pontoons. A perfect landing. I was captivated. I knew I would like this new job.

A tripod was constructed, the plane lifted, skis removed, and the pontoons installed beneath the undercarriage—ready for the next adventure.

A group of hunters from Germany had contracted with Palmer Outfitters to do a moose-hunt in northern Saskatchewan. Our days were full, preparing for the excursion. The single-engine plane loaded with food, tents, two forty-five-gallon drums of aviation gas, bed-rolls, camp stove, and fly sheets was ready for the trip. Additionally, Zane securely strapped a canoe atop the left pontoon. They flew out, fully loaded, to prepare the camp for the hunting party.

Three days later, they returned—everything was in place and ready for the businessmen from Germany. On this trip, the plane carried six people. The pilot, his brother, the three hunters, and me. My first guiding experience.

Although the plane was packed tight, the guests' excitement made the trip seem shorter than it was. The hunters had shipped over their .30-06 hunting rifles; I had my old Lee Enfield, and the Palmer brothers each had their powerful .300 WinMags. Also, they carried .41 Magnum revolvers. Outfitters were authorized to carry weapons on their hip to protect themselves from bears.

While the guests were getting settled into camp, my task was to scout out game trails that had been recently used by moose heading from the higher elevations down to the lake to feed on water plants. I located four such routes, marked their locations on a topographical map, and flagged each path's end so the hunters could identify them from the water's edge. Showing the routes became my routine each morning before the hunters departed camp for their day in the bush. I never took my rifle but instead borrowed Zane's revolver for my daily excursions. You never knew when or if you would need it. I would check the trails for recent activity and report my observations to the lead guide. Growing up in rural Manitoba and spent my free time in the bush, I was back in my element.

By the fourth day, the guests had all bagged their moose, and we were readying the camp for dismantling. I took the canoe for a last loop around the lake to pull the flags and pick up any trash that the hunters may have accidentally dropped. I untied the first two flags, tucked the yellow markers in my pocket, and paddled to the third trail. After removing the plastic streamer, I decided to hike through the bush to the last flag rather than going by water. During my drinking years, I made a lot of bad choices. But this time, I was sober.

Locating and removing the final marker was quick and easy. As I turned away from the lake edge to head up the small hill and return to where I had stashed the canoe, I heard loud splashing coming from behind. With my attention on getting the marker, I had not checked the area. A large bull moose had been feeding on water plants less than a hundred yards from the trail. And now he had seen me.

The trees in this area weren't large, but they were all I had. I ran to the tallest one I could see and grabbed a lower branch. It broke, and I fell, landing on my back and knocking the wind out of me. The colossal animal started up the trail behind me. I scrambled up and grabbed another limb, and this one held. I climbed higher. I had seen bull moose knock aside more significant trees than the one I had chosen as my refuge, so I locked onto the trunk, wrapped my legs over a couple of branches, and drew the revolver.

I'm a bit of an adrenaline junkie, but this looked like it could be a bit more than I wanted. In most situations, I felt I had some measure of control. But not this time.

The big guy stopped about a hundred or so feet away, raised his massive head, and looked me right in the eye, then lumbered forward. He checked me one more time before lowering his head and picking up his pace. If he hit the tree, I'd drop like a rock. It looked like my safe place wasn't going to be safe much longer.

The large-bore .41 Magnum Ruger Blackhawk is one of the most formidable handguns made. I had trained on the .38 Special, but this pistol was in a league of its own. As the bull closed the distance, I sighted in and pulled the trigger. The kick of the bullet leaving the barrel sent the tree swaying back as I held on to the spindly limbs. When it righted itself, I looked down, and the big guy was still coming. I knew I had hit him, but it hadn't even slowed him down. I shot again. And then again. Each time I pulled the trigger, the sway of the tree became more pronounced. Now it was bending dangerously far as it absorbed the kick of the weapon.

With the last live round in the cylinder, I fired. I hadn't taken any spare ammo, so this was it. With the tree still swaying and me uttering long-neglected prayers from Sunday school, the bull dropped dead less than five feet from the base of the tree.

Zane had heard the shots and taxied the floatplane to where I had beached the canoe. I was standing over the moose when he emerged from the brush, revolver still in my hand.

"You are one crazy sonofabitch" he said, looking at the carcass. "And now I suppose you're going to want to fly the plane home?"

"Thanks for the offer," I answered, "but I have to go and change my underwear."

# CHAPTER SIXTEEN

After a couple of more guiding and outfitting gigs, the hunting season ended. I loved the experience for many reasons: the silence and solitude of the bush, the camaraderie of other men, the "back to basics" lifestyle, and, of course, the challenge of the hunt itself. But I was now unemployed.

The work opportunities were everywhere. Businesses needed truck drivers; the Correctional Center needed jail guards, the two hotels and the Elks Club needed bartenders—no shortage of employment opportunities. I took a job as a transportation coordinator for the government. It was only a fancy name for escorting planeloads of supplies into isolated settlements on the Arctic coast. It was a new experience—riding on a canvas flip-seat in a C-130 Hercules across the tundra, hauling fuel oil, groceries, and always having a couple of rolls of movie projection film for the community.

I always looked to push myself or to try something different. So, in my off time, I took up snowmobiling. We purchased a couple of new sleds, and anytime the temperature was above -20 degrees Fahrenheit, Dee and I would explore the frozen lakes and tundra throughout the sub-Arctic.

While out on the machines, I would spot another rider, and a race would ensue. These informal races were great, but my competitive nature rose to the surface. I began to enjoy the thrill of the contest and chase the high of winning.

I began to tinker with our sleds. Changing the suspension arrangements, putting golf cleat studs on the track for added grip, enhancing the exhaust systems, and adding second, then third carburetors. All in the pursuit of speed. And I began to win. While the engine in my main sled was slightly smaller than others in my class, the tweaking allowed me to be competitive. But to win consistently, I needed more.

And so I turned to the fuel itself. While my competitors would add aviation gas or alcohol to their power mix, I took the next step. I began using nitromethane as my fuel. The significant advantage of nitromethane was that you could increase the explosive power by about eight times that of regular gasoline. If the engine didn't explode—I won. If it did blow up, I went back to my little shop and rebuilt it for the next competition. It was about 50/50 whether I would finish the course and win or blow up and spend the next couple of weeks on an overhaul. It was an expensive hobby.

My wife tolerated my adrenaline chases; however, we were now pregnant with our first baby. I had to rethink my priorities. But I wanted one more race.

It was on a Saturday. Funded by major corporations, the race drew competitors from all over North America, with a few sponsored by their machine manufacturers. This way, many of the racers had the best sleds and the best mechanics. I had my old snowmobile, a box of cheap tools, and two gallons of nitromethane. I was ready.

The race called for forty laps around a kidney-shaped course. It was a seesaw rivalry between the four top machines for the first twenty laps—two Ski-Doo "Double Eagles," a 744 Polaris "Trident," and me.

My *very* pregnant wife was two weeks overdue but still came out to the race to cheer me on. She stood on the track bank at the end of the straightaway before making a sharp left turn. I passed her position at about seventy mph. She waved, and I nodded back. It felt great to have her support. One of the Double Eagles was on the inside of the turn, and this was an excellent opportunity to take a wider path and pull ahead.

As we came into the corner, my competitor feathered the throttle to hold the inside line. I accelerated and punched my sled to the maximum.

I needed the power to hold the track on the snow, and the engine was giving it all it had. It looked like I would be able to come out of the corner in the first position.

Then the explosion.

Fully engulfed in flames, my sled lost its traction, and I went over the high bank. Between the smoke and flames and the snow pouring off the hood, I was blind. Together, the machine and I became airborne. We launched over the wall and continued through the air across the service road alongside. I landed upside down under the sled.

Dee was the first to arrive. "Are you OK?" she asked. When I answered in the affirmative, her next words cleared my muddled mind in an instant. "We have to go to the hospital. I think the baby is coming."

That was my last race.

Our daughter, Heather, was born in the Arctic, and it was time I settled down, took a real job, and made a life for my family. It wouldn't be easy, but it was something I knew I needed to do. Seeing my baby girl for the first time was an incredible experience. I needed to make some changes in my life.

I thought through the various options I had. Not having finished high school was a big drawback for any serious job search. I also knew that I needed an occupation that would provide me with variety in my work tasks. I was not too fond of office work, nor did I care for routine. I thrived on the unpredictable.

We had bought a small house in Yellowknife, and our little family settled into the predictability of domestic life. Working for the NWT Government filled my days, and renovating the old bungalow filled my evenings and weekends. I loved my family deeply. But despite the joy of being a husband and father and jamming my days with the job and nights and weekends renovating the house, I remained discontent.

Sensing my restlessness, my wife asked me the one question sitting on my mind since I'd turned in my badge. "What do you *really* want?"

And we talked. I loved the challenges of traveling to the north. The bull-moose incident with the handgun was undoubtedly a high point. And the racing was an adrenaline-fueled hobby. But the camaraderie of the RCMP and the satisfaction I got through working for something bigger than myself was something I truly treasured.

While I feared the nightmares, cold sweats, and memories of specific times and incidents, I still felt deep affection and attraction to the calling of law enforcement.

I'd been in the RCMP, and I'd been out. And being "in" was better.

Although PTSD was not in the mainstream of thought in those days, I knew that something was "off" in my life. I had read a quote from one of the ancient philosophers—Aristotle if I recall correctly. He described a "disease" that was observed in Centurions returning from battle. He called it "nostalgia."

These men had difficulty adapting to civilian life and desired to return to their unit. As a group, they had a sense of mission; there were structure and purpose, respect, and honor, and, common to all, comradeship.

That was what I had been missing. In answering my wife's question, I realized *that* was what I wanted.

The local Mountie detachment was only a few blocks away, and leaving work early on a Tuesday afternoon, I walked in and spoke to the man in charge.

Our discussion was respectful, helpful, and encouraging. As it concluded, the sergeant handed me a form—*Application to Re-Engage*.

I filled it out, adding references that included a local bank manager, the lead guide at Palmer Outfitting, and a friend who knew me well. I mailed the application.

And I waited.

A week went by. Then a month and then two months. Finally, the envelope arrived bearing the crest and initials of the RCMP in Ottawa. I tore it open.

The message was brief.

*Dear Mr. MacInnes*

*Thank you for your application to re-engage with the Royal Canadian Mounted Police. It has been reviewed, and we feel it is in the RCMP's best interests and yourself that your offer to re-engage is denied at this time. Good luck with your future endeavors.*

The force had received my application, reviewed it, and rejected me.

The news was devastating. I had pinned my hopes, my future, and even my sense of who I was on the unwavering belief that I was going to return to law enforcement.

# CHAPTER SEVENTEEN

The decision to return "to the outside" was difficult. We had made some wonderful friends, the opportunities for outdoor recreation were right up our alley, and the income we were making was undoubtedly more than satisfactory. But we now had a baby.

We needed to factor in several considerations. We took a close look at the isolation, the educational opportunities for our daughter, our career potential for ourselves, and the desire to be closer to our families. Weighted against those attributes was the uniqueness and sense of adventure the Arctic held for us. But now, having been rejected by the RCMP as a "remount," the future was cloudy.

So we uprooted once again and returned to Edmonton. But I still did not have employment.

During the following two years, I jumped from job to job. I was a cook at a barbeque joint. I peddled cleaning-supply products door to door, sold life insurance to young couples, and took a swing at being a real estate broker. I even served a stint as a security guard—five jobs in two years. Nothing seemed to click. And we were pregnant again.

The day our son, Jordie, was born was a time of overwhelming joy. Our family was now complete. We were parents who loved and honored each other, had a daughter to delight any father's heart, and now a son to cherish and carry on the family name. Jordie was born with severe health issues that required long stays in the hospital and focussed, almost obsessive care, when he was at home. And, there were times when we thought we would lose him.

But I was still adrift and despairing of my future. What was to be my legacy? What kind of man would I be, and what heritage would I leave behind? I needed more than a paycheck to pay bills and go to the theater once in a while. I needed a focus, a mission, a purpose for my life.

I was ADHD, afraid of heights, claustrophobic, couldn't speak in public, or compose two sentences that made any sense to a reader. In short, I was a loser. Or so I saw myself.

But in my darkest moment, I recalled the words spoken to me by that Mountie in Manitoba on a cold winter night so many years before.

> *"Whatever you believe about yourself, you'll become. If you think you'll never make anything of yourself, you won't."*

And sitting in that police car, with my stolen vehicle just a few feet ahead, he had talked about character, about being a man.

I had focussed on what *I couldn't do*, not what *I could*. I had to figure this out.

I genuinely believe that when we begin a realization, the universe sends opportunity our way. I call them "God Winks." We cannot ignore them.

It was at a barbershop where I always got my hair trimmed that my life took a turn. The gentleman in the chair next to me had leaned over and, uninvited, asked, "have you ever heard of Leland Val Vanderwal?"

Thinking that this must be a sports figure or movie celebrity, I replied, "No, I haven't. Who is this 'Vanderwal?'"

The man handed me a card with a name and number. "This fellow may just change your life." He then got up and left. I will never know how he sensed my lack of direction or need to get back on track. I never saw him again.

The next day I pulled the card from my wallet. *What the heck*, I thought. *It can't hurt to make the call. It doesn't mean I'm going to join some cult or something. Maybe this will be interesting.*

I made the call.

A woman answered on the first ring. Not knowing what the organization was or what product they might be selling, I hesitatingly asked, "What is this all about?"

I learned the man was presenting workshops on getting your life in order. It was to be an eight-week series conducted at a local hotel. The course cost was high, but my wife and I could attend for a bit of a discounted fee. We registered.

I learned that "Val" had been in some dark places in his life, had come close to suicide, lost everything, yet still made it back to sanity and a measure of success. That resonated with me.

The Wednesday evening get-togethers pulled a lot of information based on Earl Nightingale, Napoleon Hill, Dale Carnegie, and others. But it was a Latin phrase that caught me: *cogito, ergo, sum*. Or, loosely translated, *as a man thinketh, so is he*.

I needed to change the way I thought from expecting failure to anticipating success. Not so much the attainment of financial wealth, but having a thriving marriage, reliable and healthy friendships, and a positive outlook on life. And a significant part of that attitude was to be in a career that gave me purpose. I needed to feel worthy.

Yes, there were times I wavered and even doubted myself. But I kept myself on track with a small, written affirmation that I kept in my wallet.

> *I am entering my day with joy and enthusiasm that mounts and grows each time I wake. I am guided to say the things and do the things that will contribute to a worthy ideal.*

I would read those words every morning and at times during the day when things got rough. It became my mantra.

Stressors in life can take many forms. But some of those anxieties come from incidents or situations over which we have little or no influence. Government decisions, the weather, economic downturns, illnesses, or other people's actions—all are out of our control. I began to understand that I could only manage *my* thoughts and actions—not other people's thoughts and actions.

Although I would like to say that this was a *revolutionary* change in my life, the reality is that it was more *evolutionary*. But gradual change did happen.

I began to understand that, although the murder of my partner was traumatic and had a powerful impact on my life, it did not define who I was. Although it triggered a lot of destructive actions on my part, it was my thoughts and feelings that were affected, and those were things I had control over. But I had a sense that, in time, I would be able to talk about that night with someone who understood and without me collapsing in an emotional heap.

The government's policies and actions relating to residential schools and the Sixties Scoop would take me many more years to work out. For the present, though, I had to own my part of it. I was there. And I'd done nothing—except quit.

As I changed my way of thinking, I began to see a bit more clearly that I needed to return to policing. Rejoining the RCMP was not possible, but other forces were recruiting. The Ontario Provincial Police were in a hiring position, as were Edmonton and Winnipeg—my home city. But, rising to the top of the list was the Calgary Police Department.

Due to oil and gas exploration and development, all Alberta was boom-stage with rapid expansion in all sectors. The City of Calgary was a huge beneficiary of that growth. And they had just hired a new chief of police—Brian Sawyer.

I did my research. Brian had served for over two decades with the RCMP and risen to a commissioned officer rank. I also discovered that he had gained his education as an adult after joining the force and that he had a love of adventure and was a risk-taker. Routine work bored him, but he was innovative, a leader, and exceptionally good at motivating both individuals and teams. Sitting behind a desk was not his idea of a fulfilling life. It was a time of change in policing, and I wanted to be a part of it.

And so, I began the process.

I didn't tell my wife that I was applying to get back into police work. I think she knew and would support me, but I was worried about another rejection. Had that occurred, I'm not sure I would have wanted her to know. It would have crushed both of us.

A phone call to the personnel office was the start of what was to be a quick development. Within a few days, I received an application form. It was lengthy and detailed, covering just about every segment of my life.

There was a complete section on my recent employment and the usual questions of name, age, birthday, etc. When I listed all the jobs I had had since I left the RCMP, I cringed. They also needed to know the names and contact information of my previous employers. I didn't know if I could survive all those inquiries. More than one had been upset when I left their employ.

I emphasized my service with the RCMP and, in the interests of full disclosure, wrote a lengthy letter detailing the murder of my partner and the effect that it had on me. I came clean on the various escapades and situations in which I had found myself. But I also emphasized my strong desire to return to the profession of law enforcement.

The personnel officer scheduled me for several medicals, and there were a few follow-up questions.

Within a month, I traveled to Calgary for an interview with a selection board. At this time, I told Dee what was going on—she was delighted! She understood what I needed in my life and fully supported my action. She wasn't even upset about my secrecy around the application; she recognized why I had done it the way I did.

The selection board consisted of several sergeants, an inspector, and a representative of the personnel department. It was intense and nerve-wracking. The questions were pointed, personal, and detailed. When completed, the inspector asked me to leave and take a seat in the adjoining waiting room.

After what seemed to be an eternity, the door opened, and the inspector entered. I stood. "We have some concerns," he said. My heart dropped. "So, we've asked for another person to interview you. The chief."

*At least they didn't give me an outright no.* I walked across the street to the Central Police Station and up to the chief of police's office.

The chief's office's outer door was open, and I entered and spoke briefly to the executive assistant. She asked me to take a seat, then turned, walked to an inner door, and knocked. It was difficult to hear all the words, but I did catch the phrase "he's here."

To say I was nervous would be the understatement of the year. I was terrified. I didn't know the recruiting process, but I did understand that a meeting with the chief was highly unusual.

He stood, reached out his hand, and shook mine. "Hi, Ross, I'm Brian Sawyer. Have a seat. Would you like a coffee?"

I was immediately at ease. I shook my head no.

"How's Dee? And Heather and Jordie?"

Wow. I did not expect this kind of interview. The chief had taken the time to review my application and remember my wife and children's names.

I answered the question and expanded on my son's health issues and the desire to be back in policing.

"Tell me the story of Donny," he asked. And I did. I recounted the entire event, my sorrow over his death, and my regret that I was not with him when the shooting happened.

"When asked to interview you personally, I was curious. We don't do that very often."

I waited for him to continue.

"So, I made a few phone calls." *Uh oh.*

"I spoke to several of your former commanders. You had the makings of a good cop, but you were a drinker and sometimes out of control. You did some imprudent things that could have ended badly. Have things changed?"

I answered quickly. "Yes, sir, things have changed. I've grown up. I have a wife and two incredible kids. I want back into law enforcement. That's where my heart is."

He didn't say anything, just nodded.

"And if you accept me, I'll never give occasion to regret that decision. I'll make you proud."

He stood up, the interview over. "I'll give my thoughts to the inspector, and he'll be in touch." With that, he escorted me to the door.

I left the city to return home. My thoughts and feelings were mixed. He hadn't said "yes," but he hadn't said "no." I still had a chance.

A week later, I received a letter. I was now a member of Recruit Class #55 of the Calgary Police Service.

I was back.

## CHAPTER EIGHTEEN

But things worth doing are seldom easy. Our son was in the hospital, and Dee spent part of each day with him. And heartbreakingly, Dee's mother had recently been diagnosed with cancer. Our daughter was healthy but a very active toddler. The daily absence of her mom and the fragile health of her beloved Grandma was taking its toll.

But God is good, and friends rallied around us, handling babysitting, cooking meals, helping with hospital visits—giving us respite and courage. We were paying a mortgage on a house in Edmonton, had no home to go to in Calgary, and the training class was beginning.

Reaching out to a Calgary home-building company, I explained the dilemma I was in and asked for their help. I had learned many things over the previous few years, and a critical one was that if you need support or assistance, you should ask for it. The worst that can happen is that the answer is "No."

But Springer Homes said, "Yes."

There was a house under construction in the southeast part of Calgary that was nearing completion. They had built it as a show-home but would delay the opening for a few weeks while I found a house to buy and move my family to Calgary. They didn't put any conditions on my temporary encampment or any pressure to buy one of their new homes. They were good people helping a family that needed a boost.

I bought a roll-away bed, a couple of cheap curtains to provide the illusion of privacy, and hammered a few nails into the bearing-wall to hang my clothes. A second-hand store lamp provided enough light for my evening studies, and a giant alarm clock completed my furnishings. It felt like I was back in barracks.

As my family was still in Edmonton, and I was now living and training in Calgary, we needed a second car. So, off to Jolly Wally's Auto Sales to purchase a car so I could go back and forth to Mount Royal College, where Chief Sawyer had moved the training division. The car was a real beater—a 1963 Valiant. Push-button transmission, slant six motor, and an old piece of rusted eavestrough covered a hole in the fender. Everything rattled. But it worked. Dee retained the newer car as she needed a vehicle as much as I.

Many of the classes were similar in content and presentation to the ones I had studied in Depot. But I approached them in an entirely new way. I was determined to study hard, work hard, and succeed. The instructors were all seasoned officers selected for their expertise in the subject they were teaching. The drill instructor had served in the army; a former medic taught first aid and criminal law classes led by a seasoned officer who lived and breathed legal knowledge intricacies.

A couple of weeks before the completion of training, we bought the house where I had camped. With a letter from the department confirming employment as a police constable with the City of Calgary, and a little help from the credit union, we purchased and moved into our new home.

Graduation day came, and my wife and two children, Heather and Jordie, attended the celebration. It was a new beginning. The chief participated in the ceremony and, after the presentation of badges, approached my wife. He addressed her by name, introduced himself to our children and, inquired as to their health. He was one of those individuals who remembered every detail of each of his officers. It meant a lot to our little family, and, for Dee, it solidified the rightness of our decision to return to "the thin blue line."

Chief Sawyer was an innovator, and the commission had given him the authority and budget to modernize the policing approach. He changed the color of the patrol cars from the old black and white to blue and white. He updated the uniform, weapons, and reporting systems. His most significant change, though, came in the form of changing the very nature of law enforcement. Moving from the traditional military-based "platoon" system, he initiated the first community-centered police system in Canada and one of the world's very few.

Previously, the department had deployed officers to different areas on different shifts, seldom keeping them in the same neighborhood for more than a week or two. The chief changed things so that the officers patrolled specific districts and zones on a more permanent basis. The new "zone policing" allowed them to get to know the area's residents, visit schools and businesses, and participate more fully in community events.

The approach was ground-breaking and highly effective. Knowing the residents of an area and their concerns gave real meaning to "community policing."

But while the general approach to law enforcement was changing, the capacity for violent confrontation remained. And on a cold night in December, that dark side of the city became real.

It was my day off, and I was at home when the phone rang. It was my assigned partner.

His voice sounded agitated and stressed. "Are you watching the news?" I answered that I was not.

"Turn it on—Channel 7. There's a shoot-out in East Calgary. The guy has barricaded himself in a garage."

I switched on our old RCA television and clicked over to Channel 7. There it was—a full-scale gun battle just outside the city core. The reporter breathlessly reported from the site, and the television station showed people huddled behind cars and around buildings and poles. Every so often, a police officer would pop up from behind a barricade and fire several shots into a small white garage.

The cameraman swung his focus to a man on the ground as two officers pulled him out of the line of fire. He was dragged to a nearby ambulance and spirited away. In the next hour, through the camera lens, I was witness to three other similar scenes. Then it grew quiet.

The focus turned to the main artery coming out of downtown. There, trundling along, came a Canadian Forces Armoured Personnel Carrier (APC). It slowly and deliberately made its way to the command center outside the danger zone. While the camera showed the soldiers and police communicating, one could not hear their voices and discussions.

Within moments, the APC started up. Blue smoke billowed from the exhaust as the diesel-powered machine headed toward the garage. It rammed into the old building's north edge, collapsing the wall but leaving the roof hanging. Gunfire still could be heard coming from inside.

The tank-like vehicle backed away from the partially collapsed garage. And, once again, the officers at the scene held a conference with the soldiers. Shortly after that, the APC driver buttoned his hatch, drove forward, and collapsed the building. A man ran from the rear of the structure, and a hail of bullets cut him down. The suspect died at the scene.

Also killed in the gun battle was Detective Boyd Davidson, a twenty-three-year veteran of the Calgary Police Department. He was only the fifth officer to be murdered in the line of duty in Calgary's hundred-year history. The suspect had also wounded six other officers.

The crime-prevention model of community policing the new chief introduced was working well. The Black Friday shooting's impact necessitated another change—this one to the "crime-response" category.

Discussions in the aftermath of the shooting rampage produced several significant recommendations. A key one was the proposal to form a specialized unit to deal with future deadly situations.

Several police departments in the U.S. had already formed specialty-response units. Research indicated that the Los Angeles Special Weapons and Tactics (SWAT) program was operationally effective and could be a model to be evaluated. Calgary's executive committee sent several officers to the LAPD for orientation and training. Upon their return, they formed the basis of the Calgary Police Tactical Support Section, commonly referred to as TAC

The TAC unit consisted of two teams, each commanded by an experienced sergeant. One group was always on duty, the second on either "stand-down" or "on-call." The training was extensive and intense.

The canine unit, previously under the Field Operations Division's direction, was transferred en masse to the newly formed Tactical Support Section under the command of a senior officer. I applied for and was accepted as a police canine handler.

The first dog the unit assigned me didn't work out—he didn't have what it took to be a Police Service Dog. The next one was the winner, and he was with me for the next ten years. Pax (Latin for "peace") was the offspring of a long line of police dogs. Full coat, rich black and tan, and larger than most of his breed. He was intelligent, courageous, and athletic. At the time of our pairing, he was only eleven months old. And we would be together twenty-four-seven for the next decade.

Training for the canine unit was quite different from that of more generalized police work. The twelve-week program covered a wide range of subjects—from legal matters to canine nutrition. Scent work, such as tracking suspects, searching warehouses, and drug detection, formed our daily exercises. An instant response to commands was vital for the safety of both the dog and the officer handling him. Hours of fieldwork in criminal apprehension, learning search patterns for missing children, and working in tear gas and smoke, became part of our orientation to canine police work—a significant change from a patrol car.

And we would be working alone—just Pax and me.

## CHAPTER NINETEEN

Although Pax had a mature dog's appearance, I knew he was still a naïve pup, just over a year old when we hit the streets. His muscles had not developed as they later would, and his joints were not yet fully formed. I was careful to make sure he never jumped from too high a platform or leaped over fences or hedges.

While still in training, I taught Pax to sit calmly in front of me then, on command, leap onto my chest, wrap his front legs around my neck and hook his hind legs in my duty belt. In this way, I would carry him across any broken glass, spilled petroleum products, and even climb a ladder to a second story with him safely holding on in front. If we needed to crawl through a broken window with the jagged glass still in the frame, he would climb on my back, hold on with his feet in the same manner, and we would safely enter the burglarized building. Those techniques saved his paws from being cut by sharp objects or blistered by caustic chemicals.

While tracking a suspect, it was not uncommon for the criminal to dodge in and out of yards to hide from detection or to attempt to confuse the police dog through pulling some *Cool Hand Luke* maneuver. In that film, Paul Newman tried to foil his pursuers by leaping back and forth across a fence. It may have worked in the movie, but it certainly didn't with Pax. He just kept tracking, and I kept lifting him over each fence using his harness and line. It didn't slow us up, and it didn't require much effort for either Pax or me. He would stand up against the fence, and I would take hold of his harness; he would leap up as I lifted, then settle back down on the far side using me as his shock-absorber. It always worked.

Pax became well known for his tracking and searching abilities. Late one evening, he and I were completing a burglary call in the city's deep southeast. As we concluded the search with the culprit's arrest, a call from another canine team came in, requesting help in an armed robbery situation. A masked suspect had entered a high-end steak house and, at gunpoint, robbed the restaurant of their daily cash take. We turned our burglary suspect over to a patrol team and headed to the robbery.

The reason for calling the "Pax Team" was the challenging terrain surrounding the business. First, a fully-paved parking lot encircled the eating establishment, a major thoroughfare passed by in front, and the university campus was just a few blocks away. It was teeming with students walking back and forth between labs, residences, libraries, and the canteen. The area was so scent-heavy that it would be difficult, if not impossible, to secure a proper tracking pattern.

Knowing the difficulties ahead, I was not at all optimistic that we could help in any way. However, upon arrival, I decided to allow Pax to conduct a broad search pattern to discover if the suspect may have dropped something while running away. I planned that if, or when, we were unsuccessful, we could do some training or at least grab a coffee with the other handler-team.

For the dog's safety in this high-traffic area, I slipped his harness on and clipped a thirty-foot line to the "D-ring." I let Pax range through the lot and the adjoining regions as he wished. On a patch of grass about a hundred feet from the restaurant, Pax indicated that he had a scent source. I let out the line.

He pulled forward, nose to the ground, and crossed over the busy roadway's northbound lanes. Casting for the scent on the grassy median in the middle of the divided street, he hooked onto the track and pulled hard across the southbound lanes to a grassy field bordering the university campus.

As we crossed the field, the dog pulled harder into the harness. He neither cast around for other scents nor showed any sign of uncertainty. He had the track nailed. About a half-mile later, we came upon a small clump of willows. Head buried deep in the grass, Pax went to a stop. With his nose atop a mound of freshly turned dirt, he lay down and indicated the track's termination.

I notified the robbery unit of our find, and they quickly attended and secured the scene. Using a small shovel, a detective soon uncovered the stash. Found buried, about a half-foot below the surface, a length of rope, a roll of duct tape, a .22 caliber revolver, and two cash bags. The robbery guys were elated as they tagged and bagged the evidence. I dug around in my tactical pants and brought out Pax's old tennis ball. I threw it for him a few times—that was his reward for his efforts.

But Pax wasn't finished working.

A dozen or so feet from the hide was a set of tire marks. The torn-up grass showed the vehicle had taken off like a rocket and headed westbound through the field. Pax insisted on following the track. I let him have his head.

The dog hooked onto the tire tracks and, nose down began to follow them. It was relatively easy to catch the scent in the pastureland. It led for about a quarter-mile until a break in the old barbed wire fence showed where the tracks went through the shallow ditch and onto a gravel lane.

Pax's tracking was both impressive and unexpected. I had not trained the dog to track a vehicle. How and why he had elected to pursue this scent trail is still a subject of discussion and debate. It could be that the windows of the car were open, and the suspect's residual scent drifted down to the ground. Was this what he was following? Or it could be that there was a "transitional" moment between the footprint scent and the car tracks that had prompted the dog to continue his work. We will never know.

Whatever the motivation, I allowed the dog to continue his work. We traveled down the lane a couple of hundred yards to a parked vehicle. Pax sniffed around the car, then stood on his hind legs and peered in the driver's side window. The car was empty.

I radioed in the license number, hoping that it belonged to one of the nearby residents—no such luck. Someone had stolen the car earlier in the day. The robbery unit arrived and seized the vehicle. It was probable the robber had been the one who had stolen it. We searched the immediate area—no luck.

Within a couple of minutes, the dog located a scent trail. It led from the suspect vehicle across the alley to a fenced-in yard. I rattled the gate, but the owner had locked it. Pax stood at the entrance in his usual fashion until I took hold of his harness and boosted him over. The track continued in this manner—yard, fence, yard, fence—for about a half-block until it ended at the back door of a residence.

Detectives from the still-present robbery unit arrived at the door. When asked if I was confident about the track's continuity from the steak house to the house, I had to say yes, I was satisfied. With that, they called the TAC team, who surrounded the house. The detective had found one weapon with the buried proceeds of the crime. But there was still an even chance that the suspect or suspects were still armed.

I had pulled back from the scene not to be a distraction should an arrest be made. I would later provide evidence in court, but the Pax Team had completed its task for now.

I later learned that this was, in fact, the correct house. The suspect was a former employee of the restaurant, but the manager had fired him. He had left on unfriendly terms. When confronted by the detectives, his first response had been, "How in the hell did you find me?"

That was an almost perfect self-incriminating statement. The question blurted out before any caution or "You can get a lawyer" warning. The detective repeated the information as a part of the evidence in court.

The young man was convicted of armed robbery and sentenced to four years in federal prison.

# CHAPTER TWENTY

The radio calls for barricaded suspects, armed robberies, escaped prisoners—these I didn't find stressful. I had some measure of control over the outcomes, and I could sleep at night without nightmares. I had a purpose—albeit short-term and intense. Find the suspect, locate the child, apprehend the escapee. I would handle six or eight high-priority responses per shift. There was a defined goal—get the criminal—and that, quite frankly, fueled my sense of adventure and mission focus.

A bad guy with a gun, against a good guy with a gun—and a dog, was an adrenaline rush each night. Being a hunter/tracker was the activity I strived for in an occupation I thoroughly loved.

But I also needed to improve my skills and those of my dog. I sought out individuals who had traveled this road before me. Glen Johnston from Toronto, a world-class expert on scent work. Gerhart Schroeder from Germany, a commander with the Police Dog Section in Berlin, and Doug Deacon, a Schutzhund judge in British Columbia. These were people who added enormously to my skills and helped guide my training. They made me better.

While other families may go camping, our holidays were often traveling to other departments and organizations. I attended seminars and workshops and exchanged training ideas for the effective deployment of service dogs and, more significantly, help to the community.

As a competitive person, I entered various canine trials and contests, ranging from historical standards with the Canadian and American Kennel Clubs to the more broad-based events held by police organizations. I had a desire to improve my skills and increase the effectiveness of my dog.

By his fifth year of service, Pax was ranked the #1 Police Service Dog in Canada and had competed in over fifty competitions. He had also racked up one of the most impressive success rates of any dog in Calgary Police history.

But I knew that I also must improve *my* skills, not just in police work but also in my overall life. Just as my dog was a "work in progress," I needed to progress, as well.

I recognized shortcomings in my life. My lack of education, fear of speaking in public, and inability to articulate my thoughts held me back from being all I could be.

The impact that the RCMP officer made on me way back on that cold night at the side of the road came back now—the time I needed it.

> *"Look for what you can't do, are afraid of doing, or that other people say you can't do. Then go ahead and do it anyway."*

I began slowly. I joined a Toastmasters club, and each week would meet to learn methods and techniques to improve my speaking skills. From short impromptu talks to fully prepared and presented speeches, this changed my skills remarkably. I set a goal of being able to address a large and influential group. Later in my career, I had the honor of addressing a special session of the United Nations in New York. And it all began in the local library with a group of amazing people who met weekly to improve their communication abilities.

I took a similar path to develop my writing proficiencies. Evening courses at a local high school and a workshop with a published author were spurred by having most of my occurrence reports red-lined and bounced by the headquarters' administrators. I had the abnormal goal of collecting a hundred rejection letters for articles I submitted to magazines. But I didn't achieve it. After my forty-third submission, the *Western Producer* magazine published one of my pieces.

I had always had difficulty in traditional educational settings. It took me four years to go from Grade Ten to Grade Eleven. I needed to re-learn the way I absorbed information and upgrade my overall academic standing. I needed to do it for my family. I needed to do it for those who believed in me. But, most of all, I needed to do it for myself. I needed to erase the feelings of inadequacy that I had carried for much of my life. I started university.

The first efforts I made were cautious ones—no sciences or mathematical courses. Human resources management was something I could get my mind around as it was concepts and ideas I felt I could grasp. It took a while, but I received my certification in basic supervision skills. Now, to challenge me further, I enrolled in business management

That program was more formidable. The concepts of just-in-time supply systems, balancing assembly lines, and production analysis was away out of my comfort zone. And, the courses included sciences and mathematics—not my strong suit by a long shot. But I was determined.

The university held the courses in the evenings and weekends. If I was on-shift, the department gave me time off, and if I passed a class, they would reimburse me the tuition. For that, I am forever grateful. I would not have been able to do it without their support and encouragement.

Many of the course participants were younger students taking courses with the more "mature" students to make up for modules they had not completed. The latter, like me, were upgrading their educational standards. I enrolled in a class entitled "Linear Mathematics—The Balancing of Production."

The professor entered the theatre-style classroom and stood behind the podium.

"You are not going to like this course," he said, looking to the students. "It is one of the most difficult courses this semester. But it is one of two compulsory subjects, so whether you like it or not, you will do it!"

That ticked me off. Not just the words, but the arrogant way in which he spoke them. I stood up.

"Sir," I said. "I am thirty-four years old. I enrolled in this course so I could learn the intricacies of linear mathematics. Math is not my strong suit, but I paid for this course and am doing it on my own time with my own money. If you are incapable of teaching it, that I can understand. But it is *not* compulsory for me." I moved to leave the room. He raised his hand and stopped me. He asked me to return to my seat. I did so.

The class continued, but I noticed he looked at me several times. When the buzzer sounded indicating the time was up, the students began packing their books and moving out of the room. He came up to me.

"I must apologize," he said, holding out his hand. I shook it. "I am so used to the eighteen-year-old who is here on someone else's dime and only wants to pass the course. They have little or no interest in actually learning the contents or concepts." He paused.

"And I thank you for reminding me why I am here. To teach."

That professor became a friend and mentor, and, yes, I passed the course. And, yes, it was one of the most challenging academic subjects I had taken.

I am a rock-solid believer and advocate of the need for mentors in my life. Whether the Mountie on the highway in Manitoba, the judge who corrected me for sleeping in his courtroom, an Anglican minister, or the one I would jokingly call "the wisest cowgirl in town," they have molded my life in more ways than I can relate. And for them, I am eternally grateful.

But there is another group of individuals who impacted me in profound ways. These were lesser-known to the community, but I got to know them even better than I did the "official" mentors in my life. They were an eclectic group with diverse backgrounds, ages, genders, and former occupations. And they had only one thing in common—over the years, I had arrested each of them. But we had a deep respect and affection for each other, and their crimes were ones that they had done time for, and they were now "retired." We would meet for breakfast once a month, always sitting in the same seats at the same restaurant. They, too, became my friends and advisors.

I would take my usual spot with my back to the wall and facing the door. (It's a cop thing.) To my right would be seated an old conman. He had his peculiar code of ethics. Never swindling the average Joe but focussing his considerable hoodwinking skills on young, wealthy oil and gas executives trying to make an easy buck.

Farther over and to "Buffalo's" right was seated a fifty-ish woman who always dressed in the most fashionable style. She had run a brothel for many years but had changed her life entirely after her twelve months of incarceration. A chaplain at the jail where she served her time brought her the knowledge of Christ, and she turned her life over to living a life of character and faith.

Across the table from me was a man who I never thought could become a friend. We had fought more times than anyone I could recall. He was tough. A "street rounder" from his youth, he had become a drinker and a brawler. Through his determination to change his life, he became a long-time adherent to the principles (and meetings) of Alcoholics Anonymous. He went on to establish one of the premier honky-tonk bars in Canada. Before his passing, he had also raised over $2 million for charity.

And, always seated to my left, was one of my favorites—a retired "entertainer." This was a fancy word for an exotic dancer, which was a fancy word for a stripper. She still had a rough exterior to her persona, but she was kind, gentle, and wise. Her travels throughout

North America and her unique take on the art of stripping made her one of the most sought-after entertainers on the circuit.

I loved those breakfast meetings. And any time I needed their advice, information, or direction, they were there for me.

And in the aftermath of a horrific night beside the river, I needed them more than ever.

# CHAPTER TWENTY-ONE

I was parked on a tree-lined street, completing my notes on a recent call. Pax was snoring softly in the canine patrol car's rear compartment, having worked hard on the burglary search we had just completed. The car was quiet, with only the heater's hum operating on a low setting on that chilly spring evening. I closed my notebook and was about to put the car in gear when the radio came alive.

The dispatcher's voice was frantic. She never got excited—even for urgent or "code red" calls, but this was different.

> *"All units. All units. We have just had a call of a woman throwing children off the Prince's Island Bridge into the river. Any units close to downtown or the Bow River, please go to the shorelines immediately. The children are still in the water and moving downstream."*

I tossed my notebook onto the passenger seat, threw the car into gear, and headed for the weir. The area was a dangerous part of the river. Years before, the government had constructed a cement barrier to control erosion and aerate the water to aid in fish management. Several people had drowned there over the years, and it was to that place where the kids would most likely drift. It was quite a distance from Prince's Island, but the river was flowing fast, and it wouldn't take too long for something or someone to float this far downstream.

There was a series of barrel-floats connected by chains just above the rapids, and if the individuals were alive and able to catch one of the restraints, there might be a chance to affect a rescue. The entrance to the area near the weir was some distance from where I had parked, but I thought at the time that it was the best shot I had.

I raced over to a small public park that provided entrance to the weir. I wasn't sure if I could get close enough but had to make an effort.

The radio operator gave out additional information as it came available. A passing jogger had seen the woman park her car and get out with four young girls. Three were walking, and she carried one in her arms.

The woman, we later learned, was the mother of the girls. Along with the youngsters, she climbed the steep stairs from the parking lot to a narrow pedestrian bridge over the river. The water was raging from the late spring rains.

> *"All units be advised the caller reports that the woman had lifted one child who had her hands tied together and threw her off the bridge. She then threw the second and then the third child over the railing—a small toddler. Caller reports that the woman was clutching a fourth child—a baby—in her arms and then jumped over the railing as well. Five people in the water. The woman and four children."*

I couldn't get my vehicle close to the weir due to several barriers, so I jumped the curb and raced back to Memorial Drive, which paralleled the river, heading upstream toward the bridge. The Calgary Zoo, located along the river, had several cycling paths alongside the animal enclosures.

There was a padlocked steel obstacle blocking the entrance to a small island adjoining the park—St. George's Island. The barrier had been erected to allow joggers, walkers, and cyclists to access the paths but would prevent a car from entering.

I rammed through the obstruction, the steel pipe riding over the hood of my car, cracking the windshield. The lock on the pole that secured it to a cemented-in post came free and flew into the willows beside the barricade.

I was worried that there might be people on the trail, so I flicked my headlights to high beam and lit up the overhead flashers. I needed to ensure I didn't add to the chaos and tragedy of the night.

A small footbridge, designed to accommodate the pedestrians and bikes, crossed over a small creek. It was wide enough for the vehicle, but I was not sure it would carry a full-sized car's weight. It was a wooden bridge, more decorative than functional, and arched in the middle. I accelerated.

My car cleared the span with ease, and we traveled westbound along the path for another 200 yards until the trail dropped down closer to the waters' edge. Grabbing my spotlight, I opened the door, then released my dog from the back. I put Pax in his tracking harness and attached the thirty-foot line to the D-ring.

I undid my duty-belt, leaving my weapon, handcuffs, and other equipment on the floor of the car, and slid the portable radio into the top pocket of my jacket. We moved down the small incline and, pushing the willows aside, made it to the water.

The dim light and falling rain made vision difficult, and the beam from my spotlight was reflecting from the droplets of rain. It was a help, but not much. Water was rushing past me and the river, usually flowing gently here upstream from the weir, was now extraordinarily strong and very swift.

The radio was alive with possible sightings, new or updated information, and patrol units requesting location changes. Although we were limited to the news in the initial report, the all-out effort continued as police, firefighters, and volunteers sought to locate the bodies.

Calgary's Center Street Bridge had two levels—a narrow, two-lane roadway on the lower level and an upper four-lane road. The fire department had placed several units on the top level with their massive searchlights focused on the water's surface. Police with hand-held spotlights on the lower deck were scanning the shorelines and a small sandbar in the middle of the river.

The dispatcher's voice broke through the radio babble.

> "Two of the bodies have been recovered near the Center Street Bridge. The fire department has put their rescue boat in to help in the search and recover the bodies. There are also three paramedic units standing by—one on the north side of the river and two on the south side."

The district sergeant, responsible for coordinating the undertaking, asked, "Which two bodies?"

"The woman and the older girl. The one with her hands tied," came a reply from one of the units stationed near the bridge.

"OK," the sergeant radioed, "let's concentrate our search in that area. Focus efforts on the riverbanks from Center Street, upstream to Prince's Island."

From my position about a half-mile down from the bridge, I could see police cars that had taken up points across the river from me begin to move. They would concentrate their searches upstream near the first two bodies being pulled from the water.

As canine officers operated more or less autonomously, I had the feeling that I should stay where I was. There were sufficient patrol cars, fire and ambulance services, and city maintenance workers to cover the bridges.

I repositioned my car closer to the bank. The high beams helped illuminate farther out into the water than did my hand-held light. Pax and I searched among the willows for about an hour, both upstream and downstream, from our vantage point. The search was unsuccessful.

We stood in the water to the right of the car lights shining out over the river, positioning as best we could to view as much of the river as was possible. In this manner, we could maximize the amount of time the lights illuminated anything floating by.

A desperate search was underway along the riverbanks nearer the bridge. The fire department had their rescue boat in the water, and lights added to both the shore-based observers and the units stationed atop the bridge deck.

My eyes were getting tired, and my body felt the cold from the water, but I sensed I couldn't leave my position. I didn't know why I didn't move upstream to search with the other group. I genuinely believe that God was directing my thoughts and actions, so I didn't move from that position.

My vision played tricks on me as we spotted floating debris. A half-submerged log, a life jacket (possibly fallen from the rescue boat, or maybe thrown in the off chance that it would drift past one of the victims), and a tree branch. We waded out and checked each one.

Then, a flash of white appeared at the edge of the beam of light. It was drifting slowly past, low in the water. I began wading out with Pax swimming alongside. It was the baby, still wrapped in a small blanket. I lifted the tiny form and cradled her in my arms, and made my way back to shore. She was so cold to my touch.

I held the baby close and immediately began CPR. Her little chest rose and fell with each breath I puffed into her mouth and nose, but there was no other response. Between breaths, I radioed my position to the dispatcher to have a paramedic unit sent to my location.

As I was directing the responding units to my location, Pax began to bark. I looked to see what he was alerting to but could not see anything through the darkness and rain. I could not leave my efforts to revive the baby. I called the dog to me and unclipped his line.

"Bring it!" I commanded and pointed to the water. He disappeared between the willows, and I lost sight of him. I continued attempting to breathe life into the child—I was not about to give up.

A splashing noise came from the willows, and I could hear the heavy breathing of my police dog trying to pull something up onto the bank. It was a second child—the toddler.

## CHAPTER TWENTY-TWO

I sat there. The baby cradled in one arm and the toddler in the other. Alternating my CPR efforts between them, I would give three short breaths to the baby, covering her tiny mouth and nose with my lips. I would then shift the toddler closer to my chest and give several short breaths to her again. Back and forth I went, waiting for the trained medical folk to arrive.

I was startled by a hand on my shoulder. "I'll take over," a paramedic said, removing the toddler from my arms. He had walked in from the footbridge, the ambulance being too large to navigate the small pathway footbridge. His partner was following a police car driven by an officer familiar with the park. The units had found a more roundabout way to my location, and, within a couple of minutes, the police unit pulled up, followed closely by the ambulance.

The second paramedic took over the efforts to revive the baby, using equipment they had brought from their van.

As the two medical responders applied CPR and chest compression on the frail bodies, I could only sit on the river bank and watch. I was helpless. I knew they were going to heroic efforts to revive the two children, but it wasn't working. The little ones were not responding to the efforts made by the medics.

After failing to revive the children, the lead paramedic called over the police officer who had guided the ambulance into my location. "We're going to head to the hospital. You can drive, and we'll continue to work on the youngsters as we go." The officer nodded and climbed behind the wheel. I walked with the paramedics as they loaded and lifted each child into the rear of the van. I reached out and touched each of the cold bodies as if my touch alone could bring them back to life.

Lights flashing and siren wailing, they left the park. I began to pray. I had heard of situations where a person had been in cold water for a considerable length of time and brought back to consciousness. That was my hope and prayer.

My location, being designated a crime scene, I had no choice but to stay where I was.

I sat on the shore of the river, my arm around my dog. Members of the homicide unit and the identification section moved around, snapping pictures, taking measurements, and checking the willows for any remaining clues or bits of information that might help in the investigation.

I sat.

As the adrenaline eased from my body, my emotions began to surface. Self-discipline is a virtue, but this time it was a curse. I couldn't control my rage. I needed to hurt something, to punish someone or something. I screamed, and I swore; I tore the willows down and threw the branches in the water. My wall of self-control had collapsed. I was helpless. I had a burden I didn't want to carry, and it conflicted with everything I knew to be human.

A mother, the power of God over her children, but doing the actions of Satan, was beyond my understanding! For any human to throw four young children off a bridge into a freezing, raging river, then jump in herself, was evil.

Taking the innocent's lives in such a murderous manner was the worst act I could conceive. I had been to murder scenes, fatal car crashes, fires, notifications of death, and hundreds of other calls and tasks. I had never felt such anger and rage as I did, sitting there in the rain at the side of the river watching the ambulance take the children away.

How does one forgive something like that? I couldn't. The crime was not against me, so I had no power to forgive. The crime was against the children—and our Creator. *He* would be the one to forgive. Or to mete judgment or vengeance. It was *His* to forgive.

I went home and pushed the scene deep into my soul. I could not talk about it to anyone. I kept my feelings to myself.

My family was in bed, tucked in deeply for the night. I went up the stairs and entered my daughter's room. She was sleeping, curled up on her side, blond hair flying in all directions, and her arm around a stuffed toy she always kept close. I kissed her lightly so as not to wake her. I slowly closed the door and went across the hall to my son. He was sound asleep as well, a soft snore coming from his frail body. I looked at him in wonder and thought how very blessed I was to have two incredible children.

Finally, I undressed and slid into bed beside Dee. She opened her sleepy eyes and asked, "How was your shift?"

"A bit tougher than usual," I replied, pulling the covers up and over me. Dee knew me well, and when I tucked the blanket tight around me in what she called my "blanket burrito," she sat up.

"What's wrong?"

"Oh, we had a drowning tonight." I couldn't tell her the rest of the story—I just couldn't. I was afraid I would spiral down into that world of rage and anger that still lay just below the surface.

"I have a debriefing in the morning, so we'll figure out what happened. I'll let you know how things go." With that, I tucked the blankets tighter around me and tried to sleep.

But sleep would not come. My mind and heart were still out of control—filled with sorrow, sadness, regret—and anger and rage. But another emotion was beginning to creep in—despair.

The sadness was crushing me. Although I had been to many scenes of tragedy and chaos, nothing compared to the night that had just passed.

The morning came at last. I had not slept. I put my uniform on, strapped on my duty belt, and headed back to the station. The division commander scheduled a post-event debriefing for the morning. The on-scene officers were to share their knowledge and attempt to make sense of what happened.

The senior officer chaired the debrief, and each part of the tragedy would be examined clinically and dispassionately. We were cops. There would be no crying here.

One by one, they gave their recounting of the event. The 9-11 operator relayed her conversation with the initial caller and played a recording of the call. The dispatcher brought a taping of the radio exchanges and the responses from units reacting to the transmitted call.

When I heard my voice coming from the speaker, the sights and sounds of the night before came rushing back. For me, it was no longer an objective recounting of the facts. It was visceral. I got up and left.

I hurried down the hallway to the bathroom and threw up. I was shaking and barely able to stand. In the next cubicle, another officer was also being sick. We each exited our stall and went to the sinks to wash, rinse our mouths, and straighten our uniforms.

He turned to me with tears running down his face. "I can't take this anymore!" I nodded in agreement and understanding. He left the building and never returned to police work. He quit.

I felt the same. My conscious mind knew the risks of walking out the door. And, once again, quitting. But my emotions were on edge and winning the war for control of my life.

At that time, we did not talk about PTSD; it was "just part of the job." Although there was a psychologist on the force, there was a deep-seated belief that your career would be over if you went to see him. Management had assured the troops that this was not the case. The policy was that any visits with *Dr. Bonkers* (as the members called him) would be confidential, but there was skepticism.

Most of those affected by horrific and traumatic incidents took their thoughts and concerns to their peers, usually accompanied by alcohol and often at the back of a warehouse. Nothing shared with those outside "the circle." I was no different.

But I wanted, needed, to talk to someone.

I called my mentors. Not the "official" ones of the judge, minister, and cowgirl, but my old streetwise group. I knew they all had faced heartache, sorrow, and discouragement. None had university degrees, but each was rich in experience and understanding. We met for breakfast at our usual place.

The group was quiet. After finishing bacon and eggs, we sat sipping our second cup of coffee.

"You're down today." It was my friend, the retired exotic dancer, who opened the discussion. "What's happening?"

I related every detail of the night by the river. My race to the park, the search along the riverbank, finding the youngsters floating, and the devastating feeling of holding their cold little bodies in my arms. I shared my anger, sorrow, and absolute bewilderment that a mother could commit such a horrendous act against her children.

I wasn't looking for sympathy. I just needed to talk, and the group listened. None tried to rationalize or justify what the mother had done. No one spoke of post-partum depression, mental illness, or other possible motivations for the crime. They listened and shared my agony.

Our seating pattern at the table had not changed since the first time we broke bread together. Buffalo to my right, then around the table sat the ex-madam, the honky-tonk owner, the retired exotic dancer, and back to me.

As one, they reached across the table and laid a hand on me. One on my shoulder, two on my arm, and the ex-madam took my hand

and began to pray. There, around the breakfast table, I began to lose my anger and rage with people I had once arrested. These people could understand my emotions and not try to explain them away or give advice. They were there to listen, empathize, and support.

As she prayed, she prayed for the victim's family left behind to grapple with the tragedy—and for me. For the police, firefighters, paramedics, and emergency room doctors and nurses who had worked feverishly to save the children and their mother and ultimately failed. And she prayed for the souls of the little ones whose lives had so brutally been taken.

As she finished her prayer, we raised our heads and sat silent for several minutes. Then, with nothing left to say, we rose to leave.

One by one, each came and hugged me. Not the handshaking, shoulder-bump kind of hug, but the full-on arms around, squeeze deep and hold-on-tight hug. The "I love you" kind of hug that lifts the soul.

And Kim was the last to wrap her arms around me. Stepping back from the hug, her hands remained on my shoulders. She raised her eyes and looked into mine. The words she said gave me comfort, hope, and the beginning of a new understanding of what had happened.

*The greatest honor of your life will be to walk someone home. And that night, by the river, you carried two babies home to their Father.*

# CHAPTER TWENTY-THREE

In the weeks following the "babies in the river" tragedy, I began slipping back into that dark place of nightmares and despair. My life would seem to get back on some form of solid footing, then, *wham,* an incident such as this would push me back toward the edge. Like the officer in the bathroom during the debriefing, I felt I "just couldn't take this anymore!" And, quite frankly, there were times, particularly in the night, I wanted to quit the whole world of law enforcement.

Like so many people, I sometimes resorted to the "random chance" style of decision-making. You know, the one where you can't make up your mind, so leave the choice of paths ahead to something as mundane as "if I see a flock of geese this morning, I'll take the path on the right. If I don't see geese, I'll take the one on the left"—that sort of haphazard method of making life-altering selections

And this was one of the times I was sorely tempted to resort to one of these methods. But I didn't. I thought back to *why* I was a cop, anyway. Maybe there was a reason for all this. Maybe God wasn't finished with me yet.

I had joined the RCMP because of a lone constable on a stormy night in Manitoba. He was the standard that I aspired to achieve, but I had taken a different path. After my partner's murder, I operated in a hugely different manner from what was shown by that officer. I had become a risk-taker, a fighter, and a drinker.

After dealing with the Indian Act, the residential schools, and, later, the Sixties Scoop, I quit law enforcement altogether and headed north. It was a time in my life where I wandered. I took risks, racing anything that I could squeeze speed out of, hunting moose with a revolver, or taking long, risky trips out into the tundra. Maybe to prove something to myself or as an attempt to ward off the nightmares of my work. Whatever the reason, I'd become quickly dissatisfied with civilian life, so I'd gone back to police work—this time with a big-city department.

Through my years in the patrol division and later in the canine unit, I felt a sense of purpose—of the mission. Serve and protect was the mantra, and I did so with as much skill and dedication as possible. When I would receive a radio call, my adrenaline spiked, and I responded. The tenser a situation or, the greater the danger involved, the better I liked it.

A "code" call, such as an active shooter, a burglary in progress, a bank robbery, or an escapee from an arrest, were my stock in trade. And I loved the action.

But after the killing of the children, I withdrew. I resisted going to parties, events, or celebrations. I even retreated from my friends. But I still had my family and friends, and I was re-acquiring my faith. I became quieter, more thoughtful. Over time, I was less inclined to react instinctively and more disposed to look at law enforcement's broader picture.

It is not unusual for officers to become cynical about their work. Daily contact with violence, cruelty, injustice, and hatred takes an enormous toll on physical, mental, and emotional lives. And the revolving-door justice system that has become common in all communities seems to negate much of the efforts to control crime and effectively serve and protect. Some do their time finishing out their career and heading to a pension—some quit.

I became more aware of my development over the years as a police officer. Some were very tough and trying years. Some incidents pushed me to the edge. But, along the way, I met many men and women who helped me in ways I could not have imagined.

Mentoring has always been a cornerstone of my life. Whether I would follow their suggestions, advice, or correction was often in question, but their value to my development was never in doubt. Whether it was my grandfather who sparked in me a love of animals and horses' training, my parents who guided me with faith and love, or professors, judges, or the "breakfast club" of old street rounders—all gave me their best.

Now, if I were to continue in law enforcement, it was time to put their wisdom, so generously given, to work.

Attaining a promotion had never been one of my goals. I loved the front-line work, and to spend the rest of my career in a management position was a task I neither wanted nor sought. But if I aspired to impact the community in the way I felt I could; I needed to be in a position and rank to do so.

If I were to effect positive change in my community, I knew that I needed to be someone who could influence a broad range of decision-makers—not just those in the policing world but also the community's attitudes and approaches—a considerable ambition.

Although at that point, I was pretty vague on what changes I hoped to influence, I understood pretty well that I would not be able to make *any* unless I were able to establish some form of relationship with the decision-makers. Without a healthy relationship, they would not be open to any of my actions or recommendations.

I also felt (quite strongly) that I needed others' respect and trust for a positive relationship to flourish. These included the decision-makers in the force, government officials, the media, and influencers in the community itself.

So, how was I to gain their trust and respect? One cannot *demand* trust and respect. One must *earn* it. And how does anyone earn someone else's respect? Not by doing stuff (although that is part of it), not by saying things (although that too is a part of it), but by being a person *worthy* of trust and respect. It had to start with me.

It was by doing the simple things, like saying please and thank-you and expressing gratitude for the many blessings I had, and being kind to others. Treating everyone with respect regardless of their status, race, religion, orientation, political leanings, wealth (or lack thereof), or differences from me.

To the affirmation I repeated each day that guided my career, I now added a second part. This time it was not an affirmation but a quiet prayer to start and end my day.

I prayed for guidance to have a positive impact on someone's life. To think before I acted and to walk beside people on their journey as they walked alongside mine. And, at the end of each day, I would review my words and actions. If I'd faltered, I prayed for wisdom on how to make it right.

Was this an easy task? Not a chance! I screwed up so often and had enough setbacks I could fill another book. The "old me" kept creeping through, and I found myself often apologizing for the words I spoke or the actions I took.

But I had to keep at it. I looked at my strengths and the areas where I was weak. And while I had made strides in improving my speaking, writing, and general education, I needed more *internal* development. To uncover skills, talents, or abilities that may lay undiscovered within me. Whether or not they would ever be made public was incidental. I would find them for *myself*—not for the ego but the discovery.

I had served for over ten years as a canine officer in the Tactical Support Section. That was to be almost one-third of my time as an officer. And it was an incredible time. Many members who had service in Canine would say that it was the best years of their lives. I agree.

Now, I moved on to different responsibilities. It was not going to be a time in my life where I sought out adrenaline-pumping experiences. I still had the desire, but with a growing family and my knowledge that it was I who needed to change, I set them aside (or at least tried to keep them in proper balance.)

I was promoted to sergeant and continued working the frontlines, commanding a small cadre of officers, providing direction and leadership on a shift-by-shift basis. The dispatcher would not send me to urgent "code red" calls, but instead, I would coordinate and direct those who did. Sort of adrenaline-by-association. Not too much overtime, few court cases to attend on my days off, and more time for my family and personal journey.

I took lessons and learned to play the guitar. I set aside one evening a week to do oil paintings. I built things out of wood, steel, and stone. I learned how to smoke meat and fish and rediscovered my love of music. This journey was not a one-off but became a lifelong practice.

It was also during this time that I decided to seek further promotion. While I did have some level of influence in the department and community, my rank limited my impact—reacting to incidents, preventing crime, and enforcing laws. Could I do more?

As a family, we had, for many years, involved ourselves in the issues surrounding at-risk teens. We volunteered at group homes that housed government-ward youth. We applied ourselves with organizations focussed on gangs and drug abuse and were foster parents to teenagers whose lives had become unmanageable. Working with youth was an area of a deep passion for our family, and I felt it was an area where I might effect some measure of change.

I was given a promotion to the rank of staff sergeant. For a while, that meant that I would be off the street and work at a desk. My tasks still had close contact with the front lines as I was in an "advisory" position. This rank and responsibility provided guidance and advice to patrol officers and front-line supervisors on law and policy issues. Arrested subjects came before me, and I examined each case for its legality, completeness, and appropriate processes. Not too exciting, but a necessary part of policing.

In discussions with the department's executive, I let them know that I desired to be more directly involved in street-level work and focus on at-risk populations, particularly youth.

After an interview with just-appointed Chief Gerry Borbridge, I was offered the Calgary Vice Unit command, a section of the Organized Crime Division.

I accepted.

# CHAPTER TWENTY-FOUR

I had never served, even one day, in a plain-clothed unit. My entire time up till my transfer to Vice had been in uniform. It was a dramatic change.

The Vice Unit's mandate and function had remained relatively static for many years: reviewing licenses; conducting the occasional checkup of strip clubs and massage parlors; issuing permits; and interviewing "escorts" and ensuring their compliance with legal requirements. Part of the mandate was checking the balance of gaming tables, pinball machines, and carnival games. The seizing of lottery "gray machines" from bars and social clubs not authorized by the government was also a part of the work.

One team was assigned to check on and conduct sting operations on street sex workers, and two teams were tasked with tracking down and gathering evidence against pimps who preyed on the girls. The whole issue of pornography was shifting as society's standards also liberalized but remained part of the unit's mandate.

The seniority of the detectives assigned to the unit varied. Some detectives were newly promoted and on their first assignment. Others had been there for many years and were nearing retirement age. It's why the Vice Unit was often jokingly referred to as "newlyweds and almost deads." It was a secure position, relatively easy to manage, and the work was somewhat predictable. Few priority calls came in, and little attention or effort was directed toward exploited and abused youth.

The whole "Vice thing" was foreign to me. Over the years, I had referred several cases to them for investigation, but I'd had little contact with their actual operations. I was like a fish out of water. I needed to get a first-hand look at what the unit was doing and what my responsibilities were. I went back to the streets.

The street culture in any city is unique and foreign to most other citizens. It has its unique language (trap, stash, 5-0, bennies, flagging, etc.). It has its currency—often cigarettes, favors, personal debts, or territories. It has color codes—red and blue as a holdover from the U.S.'s early gangs, the Bloods and the Crips. The "dumpster-divers" and panhandlers had green. So, the choice of cigarette brands reflected those colors. The choice in clothing—Chicago Bulls, Los Angeles Rams, and the Green Bay Packers were also indicators of who was who and what area of town they influenced. The bike gangs wore black or clothing with black logos or backgrounds, such as the LA Kings or New Orleans Saints. It was a culture and language that I got to know well.

As part of my education, I accompanied my detectives on their calls and investigations. The time spent was not as long as I wished, but I needed to understand better the unit's scope and function as a commander.

Late one afternoon on my first week of "orientation," we covered three of the busiest strip clubs. We checked licenses, the dancers' age, the seating capacity, and that rules were posted (don't touch the girls). And we got to know the on-site managers.

I hadn't realized that the dancers were not independent but were "contracted" through one central booking agency. The agency then took a healthy portion of their earnings as commission. It may have been legal, but I felt that the dancers' control was more significant than it could have or should have been. If the girls tried to go independent or proved to be a problem, the booking agency barred them from performing. There was no appeal. And the dancers were on a circuit, traveling to different cities and different clubs, but always through the same booking agency. It was my first exposure to the "organized" aspect of the sex industry.

The escort business was confusing. There were no established standards or codes of conduct. All that escorts needed was a criminal background check from the police and a license to operate from City Hall. They would then advertise their services through various media—and that was it, they were in business!

The agency would receive a phone call from a prospective client. A "base fee" would be stated that was for escort services only—no sexual activity. However, once behind closed doors, the second set of negotiations took place. And this money was for sexual favors. It was prostitution, plain and simple.

However, as the negotiation and sex act took place in private, the Criminal Code's solicitation laws did not apply. If the premises were a hotel or personal residence, even laws relating to "keeping a bawdy-house" were not broken by the hotel or residence owner. It was a loophole that was used to significant effect. And it was a booming business.

The proliferation of massage parlors was particularly challenging. While there were many legitimate massage specialists in the city, there were also a few not-so-legitimate practitioners. All masseuses needed to show some form of training certification. The genuine ones took up to two years of training and specialized in sports injuries, rehabilitation, assistance to chiropractors, and medical clinics. But, some courses took less than a week. They all fell under the category of "certified massage practitioner."

The parlors required a city license, as well as a criminal background check. And numerous regulations attempted to govern the massage industry. The masseuse had to be fully clothed; there was no "reverse" massage, there couldn't be locks on the doors into the rooms, and several other requirements. These regulations were not put in place to control the legitimate healthcare massage specialists but to manage, as much as possible, the providing of sexual services within that industry.

The definition of pornography was changing. Once upon a time, *Playboy* magazine was considered porn, but the criteria now became blurred and extremely difficult to enforce or prosecute. Society's norm ranges between "freedom of speech and expression" and "community moral standards." The Vice Unit's detectives were required to interpret and enforce those vague definitions and community activists' push-pull.

Faith-based groups wanted aggressive prosecution. Moderates wanted it left the way it was, and freethinking activists sought additional latitude to create and sell pornography. Fortunately, we were able to get a definition from the Supreme Court that clarified the issue somewhat. Any material, video, or media that contained scenes of children, animals, or violent scenes would be considered illegal. If the item did not include those issues, then it was considered erotica and was legal.

To isolate those scenes required a detective going through each page of a movie magazine or frame. That was not a sought-after assignment. It would be repetitious, often disgusting, and always mind-numbing. On one occasion, I had assigned a senior detective to view videos seized in a city-wide raid. We had set up a separate room for this investigation.

It was a lengthy and detailed process. The officer's task was to isolate the potentially illegal scenes and mark their location on the footage for later presentation to a prosecutor. Every once in a while, another member would bring him a coffee or snack to help him stay alert and focussed.

On the third day of his assignment, mid-afternoon, I decided to check and see how he was doing. I slowly opened the door into the room. He had four televisions, playing simultaneously, each one coupled to a play-back recorder and playing out the potentially pornographic video's storyline. The detective was concentrating on a magazine on the desk in front of him. I peeked over his shoulder.

You should have seen him jump! I had startled him, and he leaped to his feet, stammering and apologizing. I picked up the magazine he had been so engrossed with, flipped it over, and looked at the title—*Field and Stream*!

I laughed. "You're supposed to be watching porn!" I said. He chuckled in response.

"After watching 136 movies, I got bored. I'd rather be fishing."

Knowing it was a task that required concentration, I had another detective take over the viewing of the remaining pile—a total of almost 200 videos. We took sixty-five to the prosecutor, he proceeded with four, and we won a conviction on only two.

Society standards had changed. Now, almost anything was permissible.

## CHAPTER TWENTY-FIVE

There seemed to be three "levels" associated with the whole issue of the sex industry. And I had spent a couple of weeks on the level that I called "licensed." These were undertakings to which various levels of government had given tacit approval: the exotic dancers, massage parlors, escorts, and the whole pornography issue.

There was a second level, which I recognized as being one of "control." These activities, while illegal and unlicensed, were regularly observed and contained by the Vice Unit. That was the whole sub-culture of street prostitution.

There were two main "strolls" in the downtown area—the "high-track" and the "low-track." Girls and women on the high-track generally dressed well, used makeup, and presented themselves more exotically than did their sisters on the low-track. The women on the low track were usually older, had suffered the ravages of their profession more profoundly, and often were afflicted with illnesses, addictions, or disease.

Several other areas of the city saw some levels of street-level sex work as well. Located in an upscale neighborhood on the edge of the downtown core was the "gay stroll." The crack-head stroll, where addicts would offer sex for enough money to feed their addictions, was located in a seedy part of the downtown east side.

Historically, my teams would develop good working relationships with the women on the various strolls. They were excellent information sources on what was going on in the city and, to no small degree, would look out for each other. Monitoring and regular enforcement were the "control" aspects of the sex industry.

The third level was one of "elimination." To this group, we gave no quarter. The unit allocated significant expenditures of time and resources to eradicating this collection of predators. They were the pimps whose sole focus was capitalizing on others' misfortune—living on the money made by the sex workers.

In no small measure, the pimps were a part of the organized-crime picture in the city. They bought and sold the girls, moved them back and forth to other jurisdictions, decided on what corner they stood to market their services, established dress codes, and enforced rules that they had made up themselves. They were a despicable subset of the sex scene.

White biker gangs controlled certain streets and corners. Asian gangs controlled others, and Black gangs controlled the remainder. Although other groups would attempt to move into the territory, they would be pushed out through intimidation or violence.

Every detective despised the pimps, and it was a significant part of the Vice Unit's efforts. But it was one particular encounter that changed the way we operated.

Although the weeks I spent familiarizing myself with the unit's operations gave me a good overview of our mandate, I was particularly disturbed about the number of girls under eighteen whom I had seen on the street.

And while there were the significant strolls in the downtown core, there was a "hidden" one that lay just south of the business district. It was tough to monitor due to its secretive nature and the participants' instinct to avoid authorities' contact. This area, made up entirely of girls under eighteen, became known as "the baby stroll."

Because of their age, they were especially vulnerable to predatory men. Their age, innocent look, and fear of contacting the police or accessing social services made them susceptible targets. The majority had ended up on the street from a background of victimization through physical, emotional, or sexual assault. They often felt that being on the boulevard was safer than the locations from which they'd escaped. And while pimps controlled some, many were "independent" or worked in groups. All were very suspicious of police contact as previous encounters had not gone well.

Over the years, several charities had formed dedicated to the rescue and rehabilitation of adult sex workers. And the three women's shelters could be accessed by those who had experienced violence and needed a safe retreat. But there was no organization or agency committed to victims under the age of eighteen.

These were the forgotten children of the city.

As in most things, you begin from where you are. That meant that when we apprehended a youngster, we followed standard procedures and returned the youth to an agency, foster care, or, in some cases, their homes. It was unsatisfactory, but there were no viable alternatives. But one incident sparked a whole new approach.

It had been a long day. You know, those times when, no matter how much you get done, there is still a mountain of work left to do. You just rearrange the pile a bit and put it over until tomorrow. I had been working late but had managed to make it home and crawl into bed before midnight for the first time in two weeks.

The phone rang, jarring me awake. I scrambled groggily for the bedside lamp, switched it on, and fumbled for the receiver. It was the night-shift commander. "I think you better come down here, Ross. The patrol officers came across something you might be interested in."

I scribbled the address on the pad of paper that's always at the side of my bed. I wasn't fully awake yet—a glance at my watch showed it to be just after four a.m. I pulled on my jeans, donned a shirt, slipped my feet into my old boots, and left the room.

Looking back at my still-sleeping wife, I shook my head. *It was the third call-out in as many weeks. I wondered what I'd find this time.*

I pulled up to the address at the same time as did one of my senior detective teams. They, too, had been called out of a warm bed—this time by me! If I had to get up, I wasn't going to be the only one. "Good morning, guys. Here is what we have so far." I related to them the information I had received as I drove from home to the site.

A young girl had escaped from a building and phoned the police. In her call, she had said how she and two others had been held against their will in a storage room and repeatedly raped. The responding officers had located the girls and taken them to the hospital. Several men had been arrested and moved to the Vice office for questioning. There was little for us to do at the scene other than look around.

What we found was like a scene from a horror film. Dirty mattresses, used condoms, locked doors, half-eaten plates of food—all signs that the girls had been held there for some time. The detectives returned to the office to interview the suspects. I went to the hospital to check on the girls.

I spent the next four hours with them. Although they were reluctant to tell their story, I sat in their room until they became comfortable with my presence. Gradually, their stories unfolded. They shocked me. Not only shocked, but their stories made me incredibly angry at the adults of the world who would stoop so low as to molest these children sexually, one only twelve years old!

It was more than assault. It was even more than rape. It was the enslaving of young children who were then used as sexual objects by adults. The emotional and psychological devastation caused to these youngsters would last a lifetime. What would happen if a particular ethnic or racial grouping were kept as slaves and used at the whim of their masters? What if this group was bought and sold for prices ranging from a few hundred dollars to many thousands? What if they had to work for no wages, in filthy conditions, and when they complained, were whipped, tortured, or killed? What would be the likely outcome?

There would be an international outcry! Every church pulpit in the world would condemn us. The United Nations would impose sanctions on our country, and politicians would trip over each other to pass legislation protecting this ethnic or racial group.

Why then do we stand idly by? Is it because they are little girls? Or is it because we, as a society, think they are making an "alternative lifestyle" choice?

After a lifetime working the streets, I still had trouble coming to grips with the sick individuals who preyed on vulnerable children. What I saw during those early morning hours made me question my sanity in taking the position as head of the Vice Unit. Maybe I should have taken a desk job. At least that way, I would not have been exposed to this garbage, and I would have been able to get my full night's sleep. Maybe? No! In reflection, this was what I wanted to do. Truth be known, it was what I felt I *had* to do!

# CHAPTER TWENTY-SIX

This incident affected me differently than others. My partner's death and the drowning of the babies gave me nightmares and other symptoms of stress-induced physical and mental torment. Why was this different? In the previous incidents, I had been helpless to prevent or impact the event. I'd dealt with its aftermath in ways that affected *my* physical, mental, and psychological health. I'd drunk to numb the memories, taken extreme risks in my work and private life, and suffered nightmares, shakes, ulcers, and obsessive anxiety. I felt helpless.

But in the kids' exploitation, I knew I could make an impact for change.

I had passed my twenty-fifth year of service and was eligible for my pension. It wasn't that I didn't need to follow policy and rules, but I was given greater latitude because of my seniority. I had gained the trust and respect of the department's senior administrators, and they approved of my intent to pursue a much more aggressive stance against the sexual exploitation of children.

I faced an unanticipated challenge—apathy. There was little concern, locally or nationally, about the fate of these kids. The standard response to my attempt to build a multi-agency team was indifference. *They made a choice. They reject any help we try to give them. There are no resources available to do anything. You're not going to make any difference anyway, so why try?* The attitude didn't surprise me. I had run into this viewpoint from the first day commanding the Vice Unit. *Who cares?*

I turned to my mentors. This time, my mentors were not the old street friends but my more mainstream advisors. Several of them were members of a luncheon club that met once a month at a downtown hotel. They would have a simple meal of soup and sandwiches, and then an invited speaker would present information about a challenge faced by the presenter and ask for feedback, direction, or advice.

They weren't a service club, religious group, or a secret society. They were a gathering of well-educated, experienced, and compassionate men and women whose sole purpose was to share their expertise and knowledge in a manner that could assist someone looking for help. I had never heard of them, although they had been meeting every month for over twenty years.

Over a bowl of Italian wedding soup and a tray of wedge sandwiches, the master of ceremonies introduced me to the members seated around tables, forming a large "U." I cannot recall all the occupations present. But there were several retired senators, a university professor, the publisher of a major newspaper, and, seated near me, my favorite mentor—the old cowgirl. Seated to her right was the retired judge who I had called on often. A podium and microphone stood in the open spot at the top of the U.

The introduction was simple, with the emcee giving only my name, rank, and position. I was allowed twenty minutes to present my dilemma. I told them about several cases that had been referred to or investigated by the Vice Unit. The recent rescue from the trick-pad in the basement of a restaurant was one of the issues I raised. I listed the funerals I had gone to, the families ripped apart, and the lack of resources to apply to this emergency. I spoke with emotion, passion, and a considerable measure of frustration. I presented the question: *What can I do?*

A further twenty minutes was devoted to the group asking me questions—and they were a tough audience!

Where did I get my statistics that ninety-two percent of the youth involved in the sex trade had experienced previous abuse? What was the annual Social Service budget for this issue? When one of them is apprehended, what happens? What is the recidivism rate? They asked for a percentage breakdown of deaths related to AIDS, suicide, malnutrition, homicide, and drug overdoses. Hard-hitting queries.

The questions caused me to back away from my frustration and anger and ask myself another: *If I don't know the answers to those questions, how will I communicate the urgency and importance of addressing the challenge?*

I could see that the stories impacted the group. I asked for their advice. *What can I do?*

Several discussions took place around the table. Some individuals would chat back and forth, share ideas and thoughts, and challenge those comments and observations. The side-bar talks continued for another half-hour.

The room grew quiet as the newspaper publisher took the podium.

"Each month, the Round Table gets together for lunch, comradery, and to engage in discussion, debate, and," he said with a bit of a smile, "an occasional argument over issues that affect our community and nation." There was a smattering of chuckles when he mentioned the word "argument."

"Our consensus today is that, while the challenge is daunting, it is vital to the community and society. You have given us a lot of information, and we can see the drive and determination you have to address this issue.

"We acknowledge that there is little community concern for the situation, and we also note there is little information circulating in the media or official bodies about the plight of the youngsters.

"After spirited discussion and debate, we offer three insights to you. What you do with this information is entirely up to you. The Knights of The Round Table is not a service club but rather a gathering of like-minded men and women who listen, debate, and share their understanding and knowledge. We do not get involved in direct community undertakings. Each member is free to pursue their interests as they see fit.

"Our three insights are thus:

1. Awareness. Before you plan or implement any project or action, the community must be aware of the situation.
2. Attitude. Once aware of the issue, you and your team can implement efforts to change the public's viewpoint from apathy to compassion, understanding, and the 'wrongness' of the status quo.
3. Action. When the community becomes aware of the issue, only then can the attitudes toward child sexual exploitation be changed. Only then can there be a process to take some form of action."

The publisher thanked me for my presentation and left the podium.

The hotel staff served coffee and dessert, and the group broke into small groups to chat about everyday things, renew friendships, and reminisce. I visited for a while, then took my leave.

Although the luncheon, presentation, and discussion had lasted barely over an hour, it provided me with a direction to pursue. I now had a basic blueprint to follow. I am forever grateful to the Knights of The Round Table members for their wisdom and insights.

★ ★ ★

Over the coming weeks, I drafted an overall strategy to address the group's three points. I stayed factual in my writing and included several instances of recent cases that remained unresolved or where the youth had returned to the street and were, once again, in danger of injury, disease, or death. I made the case that steps were needed to address child sexual exploitation in our city.

I asked for and was granted an audience before the executive committee of the police department. Superintendents and deputy chiefs attended the committee, and, for this presentation, Chief Borbridge was present.

The strategy was simple: create awareness in the community, influence a change in attitude toward child prostitution, and draw resources together to reduce or eliminate the exploitive activity.

The executive committee examines all new or significant initiatives from several points of view: human resources, budget requirements, probable effectiveness, follow-up, and agency collaboration. While I was able to address the workforce and budget requirements, the issues of success, follow-up processes, and outside agency collaboration were unknown. Despite these unknowns, I received the committee's approval.

## AWARENESS

Sometimes in police work, the media can be intrusive and negatively affect law-enforcement efforts. However, they can also be our greatest asset in information dissemination. We had two major newspapers, three local television stations, and six radio channels in our mid-sized city. And they were also extremely competitive with each other.

My team was preparing to do a sting operation on the "johns." In this undertaking, several female police officers would pose as sex workers and take up sidewalk positions in areas known for prostitution activity. The "girls" would dress in street-appropriate attire—tall boots, short skirts, over-the-top makeup, and clutch bags.

"Decoys" would be fitted with two-way radio communication systems for safety, and there would be two separate teams assigned to cover them. When the "mark" made contact and negotiated an act and price, the "john" would be arrested and charged.

Over the years, I got to know many of the media personalities. I contacted a reporter from a major daily and invited her to be one of the decoys. She readily accepted the challenge.

At the Vice office, she was fitted with appropriate clothing, wired up, and given a brief orientation on what to expect. Then we put her out on the street and drove off.

## CHAPTER TWENTY-SEVEN

Suzanne was nervous, as were we all. This venture was undoubtedly an out-of-the-box undertaking, and we were unsure how it would all shake out. The culture of the street is a closed community, with everyone knowing everyone else. Unwritten laws covered who should stand where and who controlled which corner. The "street" had a unique form of communication. Any disruption to routine would be discovered quickly, and the knowledge would be shared with the others.

It seems counter-intuitive to an undercover operation, but we informed the regular sex workers that we would be conducting a sting operation. With few exceptions, they all supported the initiative, and some were happy we were going after their "customers." Some provided specific information about johns they wanted us targeting because of violence, rudeness, or demeaning language. It was a fascinating interchange. The "regulars" pulled back from their usual spots, allowing our decoy to work unimpeded.

We had selected a spot near a low-wattage streetlight. The flickering glow was sufficient for our cover teams to maintain surveillance on Suzanne but dim enough to create the atmosphere of a low-track gal looking for tricks to pay her drug dealer and pimp.

She was new flesh on the track, and it wasn't long before there was a lineup of cars wanting to negotiate a deal with our decoy. Two senior detectives had schooled Suzanne on how to negotiate and how to rebuff their final offer. We would not allow her to enter a car or get within reach of a man seeking her company for a quick trick.

Monitoring radio communication was fascinating. "Are you a cop?" was a common question, and our gal would honestly and sincerely reply, "No." Often, the mark would ask for more information, such as where she was from, how long she had been "working," or what her specialty was. What immensely angered Suzanne was that she had seen two cars that had baby car seats in them and, shockingly, one man had a child in the rear seat.

The operation was ending, and we were getting ready to pull the reporter from her position and go for a late lunch and debrief her experiences. However, there was one more encounter we believed she needed to understand—a confrontation with a pimp.

One of my undercover officers looked like a rough-and-tumble biker—long hair, scraggly beard, blue jeans, and leather vest. He was driving an older, unmarked police car we had used as one of the observation posts. He pulled up alongside her.

Sliding over in the seat, he kicked the passenger door open and yelled. "Hey, bitch! What are you doing on my street? And where are *my* girls?"

Before starting the operation, we had given Suzanne a "keyword" to say if she felt in danger or needed rescuing for any reason. The word was "toothbrush." Now she had the chance to use it.

As the detective harangued her, she nervously moved back along the sidewalk. When Brent told her to get in the car, she replied, "I can't, I have no toothbrush." It was the agreed-upon signal, and I knew she expected us to rush in and defuse the tense situation. We continued our silence, knowing she was safe but wanting her to have many of the sensations that other street gals experienced.

As the reporter became more afraid, she sped up, saying the secret word. "I need to get a toothbrush! A TOOTHBRUSH, TOOTHBRUSH, TOOTHBRUSH."

After a few minutes, the rest of the cover-teams drove over and "rescued" her. And she got to meet Brent as a detective, not a biker pimp.

"That was the scariest thing I've ever experienced," she exclaimed as I drove up. She was a tad angry with me for setting her up, but after calming down, she understood that this was a nightly occurrence for the other girls working the street, and now she had a glimpse into their lives. It was not at all glamorous like *Pretty Woman* or other movies that glorified prostitution.

Two days later, Suzanne published her experience and produced a radio news report on the incident.

That was just the opening round of our attempt to bring awareness to the city.

## ATTITUDE

The second phase of our campaign was to shift the attitude of those entrusted with these kids' care. We held workshops for teachers, social workers, parents, funding organizations, and service clubs. We pulled out all the stops in our drive to inform the public of this underground sexual exploitation and abuse.

We spoke at high schools, churches, community events, and social agencies. A program entitled "High Heels and Teddy Bears" was developed to inform the public of the tragedy and misery of the youth involved and their families. Workshops were held in local hotel ballrooms and attended by a wide variety of folk.

In these workshops, we had parents, youth, and investigators speak to the issue. On one occasion, we were able to convince a pimp to share his story, as well.

We opened up our efforts and invited community leaders, politicians, and news reporters to ride along with my officers and get a first-hand look at the conditions on the streets. We needed the help of those in authority to move legislation forward and secure resources to address child prostitution's heartbreak.

Over the next year, we made appearances on television talk-shows. It was challenging to arrange for local talk shows, so we went international. We contacted several talk shows filmed in New York and invited them to share the story on a bigger platform than we could have managed in our city. Bill Curtis of *A&E's Special Report* did a one-hour exclusive. We brought in parents of the youth to relate their terror of having children on the street. Girls who were now over the age of eighteen and had been on the child prostitution "kiddy stroll" told their stories. News that the media had never reported.

Although the subject was somewhat controversial and was, without question, uncomfortable, the senior administration of the department supported my efforts. They fielded all complaints and continued backing our campaign.

During the second year of our efforts, the death of "Billie" made a tremendous impact on me. After her diagnosis of AIDS, we made a significant effort to move her to a rehabilitation facility. It was unsuccessful. Our efforts at rehabilitation were rejected—not by this fifteen-year-old but by the system itself. There was no adequate legislation in place, nor was there any dedicated program or service through which we could safely and effectively bring her back into a regular teenage lifestyle.

As we went into the second year of our campaign to increase awareness and shift the community's attitude, the issue reached government consciousness. It was this poem that I penned in a time of discouragement and personal anguish that prompted action.

## THE BATTERED DOLL

With smudged-on rouge and dime-store rings
She strolled the street that night.
Her only toy a battered doll
As she walked beneath the light.

We saw her as we drove the street
Our thoughts were on our child.

## SHADOWS COME AT MIDNIGHT

Who, but for God and circumstance,
Could be right there. We smiled.

Our smugness was a cozy wrap.
*Not my worry,* we thought then.
She chose the life, the street, the trick.
She could go home again.

We passed her by, no backward look
To see the other car
That picked her up and drove her off
Her very soul to scar.

Two years went by, and then we saw
Her once again—that's all
It took to see those track-marked arms
Hold tight that battered doll.

At the curb, I stopped and called her name
(She's on my list, you see).
With HIV, we had no choice
And so, she came with me.

We sit on polished pews today
And view the casket there
She looks so young—no worries now.
No trap, no stash, no cares.

The preacher talks, the choir sings
There's a cross up on the wall
And laid across the little girl,
There's a battered, broken doll.

The men still drive those streets at night
As she rests beneath the sod
From the little child, they tore the soul
And broke the heart of God.

# CHAPTER TWENTY-EIGHT

Through efforts to inform the public about the existence of child prostitution in the city and the shifting of attitude toward the youth—numbering over one hundred at any one time—we began to hear a call for action.

## ACTION

Almost from the beginning of our campaign, we saw measures discussed. Some steps were taken quickly and integrated into existing programs. These included invitations to give regular talks to the forensic nurses' studies at the university. Those presentations' focal points were identifying and dealing with victims of pimp-controlled child prostitution.

The stories of the street were collected in book form and published through Friesen Publications. A grant from the Calgary Foundation enabled 20,000 copies to be published, and a large electronic company arranged to send the books to schools, libraries, and universities across Canada. *Children in The Game* achieved best-seller status within a month of its publication.

A commercial film company volunteered to produce a documentary on two of the stories. The twenty-two-minute documentary, entitled *The Butterfly Collectors*, won several awards, and its debut at a downtown theater drew over 300 attendees.

With the department and several social agencies' support, we initiated a new street outreach. The program personnel was a mixture of retired police officers, ex-street sex workers, and community volunteers. The outreach was coordinated through the Vice Unit and named "Street Teams." The intent was to use innovative ways to contact the youth, establish trusting relationships, and arrange processes to get them off the street and into long-term rehabilitation programs.

The Royal Canadian Legion donated a van, and a local car dealer provided an older sedan for the volunteers. The police department provided oversight and core funding for the project. Things moved quickly.

One of the effort's core principles was that the team members would take nothing to the streets except their knowledge, compassion, and determination. The teams did not distribute gloves, clothing, food, condoms, needles, or anything to facilitate the child staying on the street for one more day. If a child was hungry, we took them to a restaurant or a fast-food outlet and provided a meal. If they were cold, we took them to a place of warmth and safety. Each contact was an effort to create an attractive alternative between the street-life and the straight-life.

Existing social agencies, working side by side, created a "safe-haven" at the local YWCA. This undertaking enabled the teams to contact, befriend, and provide a protected place to receive warmth, medical help, clothing, and initial counseling service. It was successful. However, there were some flaws in the process.

Because there wasn't any form of legislative authority, the young person was free to leave at any time. And the call of the street was sometimes too loud for them to resist. What was needed was a new provincial act, specifically written to protect the youth at risk.

Solicitor General and senior member of the Alberta Legislative Assembly (MLA), Heather Forsyth, took on the job. She drew together experts from across the province. As a part of the task force, we met monthly to examine the issue and draft legislation.

And Alberta's Premier, Ralph Klein, not only supported the undertaking but presented it as the primary bill at the next sitting of the legislature.

The Protection of Children Involved in Prostitution (PChIP) Act became law. It was the first piece of legislation created and solely dedicated to eliminating the scourge of child prostitution. It was highly effective.

The Act allowed officers to apprehend a child at risk and place them in a secure, safe environment for a short time to enable resources to be tailored explicitly to that youth. It took fewer than three months to see a significant change. Underage youth on the street dropped from an average of a hundred per night to fewer than a dozen.

Because of the background and lifestyle of the children, their education had been cut short. None had finished high school, and many had not even completed Grade Eight. Their chances of finding a legitimate job were minimal. We needed to create a new approach.

Working collaboratively with the Board of Education, several psychologists, a medical doctor, and two other social agencies, we evolved a plan. The former Children's Village, an older complex that had served its time as a youth-development center but was now mostly vacant, was ideal. The students needed a specialized curriculum, educational material (purchased or sometimes scavenged from other schools), and two board-certified teachers.

There were also a couple of unique features. First, all the students were from the at-risk population, so there was a commonality among them. The girls' shared background also presented its unique challenges, as many came from recent contact and control of rival gangs, which carried over to the school setting. The second distinctive element was in the hours of operation.

While the mainstream school system had a start time of 8:45 a.m., this proved challenging for the population we were attempting to reach. The sleep patterns they had developed made it difficult for them to attend any form of "regular" schooling. Their chaotic lifestyle was certainly not conducive to sitting at a desk and studying Shakespeare.

The classes would begin at noon after a nutritious lunch and continue until 5:00 p.m. There were no desks; the kids sat on the floor, used stools, or accessed one of the dining tables scattered through the room. It was informal, inviting, and low-pressure. The long-term goal was to have the youth ready to enter the mainstream system and complete their education.

The innovative approaches were not successful on all fronts. There were ongoing issues of drugs, gangs, and emotional/mental challenges. Some dropped out of the school through pressure from their street friends. "You've squared up, and that's not cool," was the siren song that pulled them back to the street. Others were unable to deal with the limited structure of daily classes and left. But most remained and successfully transitioned into the more traditional school settings. Many eventually completed their high school, and several have gone on to university or community college.

But what about those we were unable to reach?

Each night, two fifteen-year-olds would stand together at the entrance of a gravel parking lot next to a church for safety and companionship. Their "home" was on the street, standing in the dark, waiting for a paying john. And one night, Karen disappeared.

We have a family policy that any youth can phone us anytime, anywhere, for any reason. We would always take the call, which would often be "collect." We always said "yes" to receive the charges.

We received three calls from Karen, one from Toronto and two from Montreal, and we talked for hours in an attempt to bring her back to Calgary. She was under the control of a particularly vicious pimp—an illegal immigrant from the Caribbean. Her final call came at two a.m., on August 14, a Sunday morning.

"He's going to kill me," she sobbed through the phone.

I asked, "Why?"

"I had an abortion on Friday," she murmured. "And he wouldn't let me take the evening off. He put me back out and demanded that I turn in $800 in tricks for the night. I was so sore!"

We believed her. We knew from the call-source that she was in a Montreal suburb but could not get information about her actual address or location. I don't think she knew herself. I asked her to smash a window, steal a car, do anything to get herself arrested. We would be able to sort out the charges and bring her back to Calgary. She agreed.

But then, we heard a man's voice in the background, and she quickly hung up the phone. We never heard from her again.

The following morning, I was at my desk in the Vice office. The phone rang. It was a detective from the Laval police department in Quebec. "We've located the body of a young girl behind a dumpster in a shopping center," he said. "And your business card was tucked in her bra. I thought you should know. Her name was Karen Lewis, and she has been murdered."

Her death was particularly devastating to us and to the new programs we had initiated. Over the years, we had lost several youths to tragedy, but this death was different. We were so close to getting her back. And we failed.

We had to do more. We needed to intervene at earlier stages before the girls were lured to the street. Contact needed to occur when they were engaged in high-risk activities but had not yet been coerced into the world of child prostitution.

How could we compete with the call of the street? What could we do that would provide the sense of family, safety, acceptance? And, yes, we also needed to include the adrenaline rush that "the game" provided.

Growing up around horses and through my background with the RCMP, we felt that maybe, just maybe, we had a possible direction on which we could embark: a long-term, residential program staffed with knowledgeable, dedicated people. The plan would include an equine component that would be key to reaching those hurting hearts.

# CHAPTER TWENTY-NINE

It took a year of focussed effort. We met with parents who had lost their children to the streets. We engaged in many discussions with social services, legal experts, and Parliament members and audited programs throughout North America that seemed to be effective in reclaiming the kids' lives.

And we had to raise over a million dollars to start the ranch.

My wife Dee and I faced a decision. I was due for another transfer. It was a standard policy to rotate commanders through various responsibilities, and my time in Vice was ending. Did we accept the transfer to the homicide unit? Or a district command? Or an office position or promotion to a higher rank?

Leaving the Vice Unit was not a transfer that I sought, nor was it one I wanted. We had successfully combatted the evil of child exploitation and had developed plans for the long-term residential program to catch high-risk youth before them being coerced onto the street or into trick pads; I wanted to continue. But policy dictated otherwise.

So, after thirty years in all facets of law enforcement—front line patrol, courts, jails, community policing, intervention, apprehension, and influencing change. I retired.

★ ★ ★

The ranch development was a unique challenge and one for which I had no training or background. Raising money for constructing a 13,000-square-foot house, the outbuildings, horses, trailers, feed, and all the things necessary to set the effort in motion took a full-on struggle.

We gathered around us a group of incredible people, including politicians, parents, corporations, foundations, engineers, and our own family. The energy and excitement were extraordinary. And, within the second year, we opened.

It was a unique program. Upon arriving at the ranch, the youth and a qualified adult paired together. The adult would mentor them through their year at the ranch. Also, we employed two psychologists and had under contract, a psychiatrist and a wrangler. And while the program model was influenced by organizations in the U.S. and Canada, the integration of horses into psychological therapy was new and innovative.

A vital principle of the program was that we had a "heart-side" that needed healing. At the same time, the center was not a "religious" organization. The counseling recognized that loneliness, fear, anger, and violence were not just physical acts but rather a disconnect from the Creator. We acknowledged God as the source of healing for broken spirits.

Teenagers, in their often-chaotic years, need three things. First, they need to sleep. The hours of operation began with a "boots on" rising time of ten a.m., rather than the usual residential program time of seven a.m. This late "get-up" allowed the youth to achieve a more natural rhythm to their rest and eliminated many of the challenges associated with waking a teenager in the morning. "Boots off," when the youth had to be in bed, was set at midnight.

The program model also recognized that teenagers need to be a bit defiant of authority at times. In speaking with the staff and parents, we would remind them of their own teenage lives and their conflicts with parents, schools, churches, or legal authorities. That did not mean that the Young Riders (as we called them) were permitted to become violent or destructive. Instead, they were allowed to fully express their frustrations or anger without fear of punishment or retaliatory action from the staff.

A component in the program model acknowledged the third need of a teenager: the need for risk. Again, we reminded the staff and parents of their teenage years and some of their chancy behaviors. Whether it was jumping off a railroad bridge into the river, speeding in a car, or getting involved in petty crimes, the need for an adrenaline rush was a part of growing up. Horses provided that rush.

And horses were an integral part of the therapy. Each girl, upon arrival at the ranch, was introduced to the horses. And, differing from other programs, ours had the horses select their partners. The introduction was unique and meaningful. The herd of horses was let loose in a large field, and each girl was encouraged to walk into the grazing group of animals and get to know them. The youth would pet them, talk to them, tell them their struggles and worries, and learn of the horses' backgrounds and how they came to be the ranch. Without exception, each Young Rider would walk out of the field with a specific horse following them. There just seemed to be an incredible connection between that particular horse and the youth.

Whether it was racing along trails, splashing through creeks and rivers, or just sitting quietly on the back of the horse while talking, the integration of horses into the program was magical. We began to see change happen. It was sometimes in small ways, sometimes in significant respects, but transformative change always happened.

In the early days, quiet times of prayer and reflection were vital for each development stage and, later, each program undertaking. Volunteers had stepped forward to build, repair, and maintain. The staff took their lead from me, and the young people took their direction from the team. It was truly magical and inspiring.

The ranch became a symbol of success. Support from politicians was growing, and community leaders were becoming involved. It became common for my wife and me to receive invitations to sit in private boxes at NHL games, attend exclusive concerts, be a part of fashionable committees, or sit on corporate boards of directors.

It was heady and ego-gratifying. But it was also distracting me from my mission and purpose.

And, over the years, something else was occurring. As the ranch grew in client numbers, so did the complexity of my role. From working almost full time with the youth and the horses, I slowly yet inexorably became more involved in the organization's administration. The need for regular and predictable funding compelled me to spend three or more days a week in the city. I met with foundations, business leaders, corporations, and other funding sources to keep the ranch operational.

An annual budget of almost one million dollars necessitated a constant flow of income. And with each commitment for funds came a subsequent requirement for administrative reporting. I spent long hours at the keyboard relating outcomes of the programs, disclosing expenditures, writing reports to the government, and planning for the next round of funding applications. I found I was spending less time with the youth and more and more time producing reports that I genuinely believe, few even read. It was just part of the system.

As fame grew along with the necessity of my being absent or in meetings, the endeavor's effectiveness began to suffer. Success rates dropped, staff began to lose enthusiasm, and, although the view from the outside was impressive, the program also began to suffer.

Slowly, funders began to withdraw, and the famous didn't come around anymore. In the early years, we started each day with prayer. But no more. I was now presenting a proposal for additional funding in some corporate office. Instead of working with the staff and youth in the afternoons, I compiled reports for the government.

I had lost my vision and neglected my mission. I began to focus more on the money we needed, and from whence and when it could come, than on the purpose of the ranch. *I* had left God out of the equation, but *He* hadn't left me out of His.

I began to blame politicians who had pulled their support and funders who reneged on their commitments. I was discouraged, annoyed, and slipping back into my old "angry" role. I needed to re-set my priorities.

And so, I went down to the horses.

Caddie was a grade horse, meaning he was a mixture of several breeds. Stocky, powerful, and determined, he had a majestic bearing and a "way of being" that drew respect from the rest of the herd. Maybe he wasn't the traditionally viewed "herd leader," but he certainly was a presence and influence on the horses' entire band. They willingly followed him in whatever fashion he desired.

His early background was a working cow-horse, but he loved tossing people off at the most inopportune times. We never thoroughly learned *why* he did this, but he never changed. He was one of the earliest horses to arrive at the ranch. Due to his penchant to buck a rider off, he was deemed unfit and was about to be put down. But the owner had heard of the ranch and offered him to us at no cost. He became my horse, my confidant, and my friend.

And he loved to work. Each time I went down to the pasture, there he was, waiting for me. Whether on the trail, breaking through deep snow, or dallying another horse, he was always up to any task I requested. And on that day, I needed him to talk to me.

As I stood beside that beautiful animal that morning, pouring my fears, anger, and hurts into his mane, he began to speak to my heart. He had gone through a time of anger and bitterness and, at times, even his soul had shut down. But working alongside the kids and me, he had regained his purpose and love of life. He gave from the heart.

The warm breath of the horse and the ache of knowing his story broke through to me. I could see my life reflected in his eyes. It was a re-awakening of my purpose.

I had to get back to the objective—working with the youth. I had become distracted by fleeting fame and the focus on raising money and filing reports. I needed to get back to what I felt God had called me to do.

I stepped aside from the role of the leader of the organization. I didn't resign from the mission; I just left the distractions.

# CHAPTER THIRTY

I took a brief hiatus from my work. I needed to reflect, renew, and re-energize my life if I was going to be effective. I knew that administrative tasks, although necessary in any endeavor, were not where my heart lay. I had spent my working life on the front lines, and that is where I felt I belonged.

Over the years, I had continued my education, gradually building my knowledge. I took university courses at night and studied abnormal psychology, adolescent behavior, sociological impacts, and even a semester on philosophy. I wanted to more fully understand the long-term implications that traumatic incidents had on a person and the process of recovery.

And, being a horseman, I knew the power of the horse to heal broken hearts and imbue with courage those who lived in a world of anxiety and fear. I had seen the transformative impact of equine-assisted psychotherapy on the youth and families at the ranch. And, although I had allowed myself to drift away from being an integral part of that process, I strongly felt that I should return to what I knew and loved—the magic of the horse-human connection. But I would not be returning to the treadmill of funding, administrative tasks, and filing reports. I would focus on the mission, not the process.

Once again, I started over—this time, with no land, buildings, tack, or horses. But my vision had cleared, and my mission strengthened. I went back to basics.

Although we had concerns about starting over, we approached the challenges with optimism. Leasing appropriate grazing land wasn't hard, but the barn that was part of the property was a problem. It was filled to the rafters with old furniture, used equipment, rolls of barbed wire, and boxes full of stuff we couldn't even identify. The floor was gravel, many of the windows broken, and the doors wouldn't open or close without a significant effort. But the roof didn't leak, and it had electrical power. It was a start.

The day we began to clean it up, the task seemed overwhelming. Maintaining our optimism was going to be difficult as we faced the daunting task of sorting, saving, disposing of, moving, or doing dump-runs with the mounds of junk left behind by a previous tenant. There were items quickly decided upon as dump material—a roll of old carpet, frayed and moth-eaten horse blankets, an easy-chair with a broken leg, and several pails of used oil. But what to do with a wood-burning kitchen stove from the 1920s? Or lengths of aluminum pipe from an irrigation system that had last seen use thirty years before? Decisions, decisions.

As we dug into the mountain of trash, we heard vehicles pull up outside and doors slam. "Hi, guys!" voices sang out as the old doors swung open, and a dozen people entered the dim interior. It was our old graduate families from the residential ranch who had come to help us. What an honor.

Every day for two weeks, the group would arrive and get to work. Pickup trucks loaded with junk moved back and forth to the local dump. They built racks to hold the lengths of pipe and steel, repaired windows, and rehung doors. Using old lumber, leftover poles, and rolls of wire, the volunteers constructed a hayshed, erected horse shelters, and rebuilt fences. The property owner, delighted to see the old barn and pastures' transformation, gave us three months' free rent! We were ready for a re-start.

When we had made known to the board of directors at the previous residential ranch that we were going back to basics, they made the generous offer to provide us with six horses that had been "in training" at the center. While these horses had some behavior problems, we accepted them with thanks. There is no such thing as an untrainable horse. Like people, they have backgrounds and challenges that need to be understood and accepted. Once they are, the animals can become great riding horses that also serve as outstanding therapy horses. Included in the generous donation was my horse, Caddie. The board knew my connection with him and was, I think, relieved that we accepted him as part of our new herd. The book—*I Am Cadillac—Life Lessons from A Horse*—would feature this incredible animal.

In the ensuing months, the more focused and dedicated approach to high-risk behavior in youth began to show the same positive results as the residential program's early years. But this time, we operated the ranch with no outside fundraising or complex administrative processes. I was able to give full attention to working directly with youth and their families. We recruited volunteers and provided training in running the new ranch and working with the horses. Many of the helpers took additional training to understand how horses contribute to psychological healing, and our "staff" of unpaid workers continued to grow. Our small collection of six original horses developed into a herd of over forty.

It was never our intention to develop into a more extensive program model. Still, the undertaking's continued success drew interest from other individuals and groups who had hoped to develop similar approaches. It had three critical components of a repeatable format. First, it was successful. Second, it was affordable, and third, it had little red tape and few hoops to go through.

But success comes with its challenges. As a species, humans have an instinct to prepare for something to go wrong or to fail. But we seldom give thought to the possibility of "What if we're successful?" As the reputation for effectiveness grew, so did the demand for client services. The youth component quickly expanded to working with families. With trauma survivors, people living with early-onset dementia, and people suffering from several other oft-neglected areas of the human condition.

How does one replicate any endeavor? How could what we had done be taught or imparted to others? That question became a focal point of our prayers and efforts over the following couple of years. We had not intended to grow the program or expand into so many areas, and we had enough work at our ranch to fill our days and weeks.

But it seemed that God had other plans, and one spring morning as we were preparing for the day ahead, we received a phone call. Would we be willing to work directly with a First Nations community to initiate a similar program? Without hesitation, we said, "Yes."

It was a daunting task. The community had an old abandoned ranch on the northeast corner of the reserve. Fences were down, and the buildings dilapidated and, a significant problem—there were only feral horses with which to work. And we had not trained anyone in equine-assisted learning (EAL).

The challenges presented were numerous. Teach the science behind EAL to others, recruit more volunteers, repair and renovate the old homestead on the reserve, round up horses to use in the program, arrange transportation for students, work with the band council and elders, and map out the daily activities for a twelve-week program. All this, in addition to maintaining our ranch and client work.

But our "team" came through. Volunteers from the home ranch stepped up and took over the tasks at our place. Contributing to the effort was the commitment of the residents of the community itself. Dozens of First Nations members came and pounded posts, created a training and teaching area, repaired the old buildings, and hauled in loads of hay that would see us through the three-month schedule.

The program began with us trailering in horses from our home ranch. But that didn't last long. Within the first week, the new students and helpers from the home ranch rounded up twenty feral horses. It was an all-day effort to locate and move that large herd from the reserve's bush and foothills to the newly prepared corrals. Slow and steady was the plan, but moving wild horses is nothing but an exciting undertaking. Adding in a couple of trained "loaner" horses from friends, they became the program's backbone.

It was a new experience for me. An elder opened the program with a sweetgrass smudge and earnestly requested the Creator to bless those participating and give wisdom, guidance, and understanding to the leaders. As the fragrant smoke wafted through the group, there was a deep sense of harmony and purpose.

Smudging is a ceremony that is common amongst many First Nations. It involves burning sage or sweetgrass and "washing" oneself in the smoke rising from the smoldering medicine. Participating in the smudge creates an atmosphere of calmness and focus.

Led by the elder, several senior members of the band held a special ceremony for the horses. The herd, now numbering almost thirty, was let into the main arena-sized corral. A quietness settled over the assembled group as an elder stepped forward and raised his hands. And, as the horses milled around, the *Singer-to-the-Horses* began his song, and the drums began to sound. The horses started to move. These magnificent animals seemed to sense the ceremony's reverence, walked the perimeter of the corral, and then began to trot. And from the trot, they began to gallop, first slowly and then with increasing speed as the drums' beat started to change, the singer's voice growing stronger. I stood in awe.

There is only one singer in a First Nations community with the words to the *Song To The Horses*, and he sang with such power and devotion. As his voice trailed off and the drums became muted, the horses stilled. Then, as in a dreamscape, one by one, the horses lay down. These were feral horses! But the song and the drums brought a calmness and peace that I had never witnessed. What a start to the program!

It has been our honor to be a part of several equine-assisted learning programs for First Nations communities in the ensuing years. The reverence shown to the horses and the understanding of their role in Aboriginal culture is not present in other equine endeavors. It is truly something special.

Despite the incredible experience of leading courses in First Nations communities, I felt a sense of discomfort. Many students were children or grandchildren of those taken off the reserves and sent to government-sanctioned residential schools. And three of the students had been directly affected by the Sixties Scoop.

I did not reveal my role in those injustices. That would be for another time and in another place. For now, I carried my conscience in silence.

## CHAPTER THIRTY-ONE

The EAL portion of our work continued to grow. In addition to working directly with First Nations communities, we conducted workshops and training throughout Canada. These five-day courses began to change lives—not just in the clients our students counseled, but in the students themselves.

A part of our teaching was on the long-term effects of traumatic incidents. Whether it was a single harrowing event that deeply impacted a life or a series of events, people's deep desire to identify and come to terms with the incident was real.

We shared what we had come to learn about the many ways horses helped heal and to focus on the long-term effects of post-traumatic stress disorder (PTSD). Many of the students had suffered traumatic incidents throughout their lives, ranging from sexual assault to witnessing the murder of a family member. And the course began to attract attention from military and first-responder organizations.

I researched the historical origins of the condition and society's tendency to change its name over the years, from "shell shock" during WW I to "battle fatigue" during the Vietnam War and the now everyday use of PTSD. Historically, the term referred to those in the military. But more recently, it started to be used to describe the psychological symptoms of those in civilian front-line work.

My presentations and teaching were more of an intellectual exercise than personal experience, but there was a noteworthy turn of events during one course.

Dee and I were conducting a week-long course at Heavenly Acres in Ontario. It was a successful class with a full complement of students and some magnificent horses. Mid-week, a physician specializing in PTSD asked if we would be willing to spend an extra day demonstrating the significance of a horse used in a therapeutic approach for her patients. We agreed to provide the time and demonstration.

The evening before the presentation/demonstration, we attended a fundraising event supporting PTSD research and recovery. The room was packed. First responders told stories and startling statistics shared by the presenter about the numbers and trends of suicides, drug abuse, and mental health issues. Some were having a silent effect on me.

We had anticipated conducting demonstration exercises and explaining EAL's role to the doctor and a few therapists for the following day, but that would not be the case.

I had prepared my talk and explanation for a group of professional therapists. Using the horses at the center, we conducted demonstrations that illustrated the various stages people living with PTSD experienced after a life-altering incident occurred. I was ill-prepared to present the information and demonstration to actual patients.

Before beginning the presentation, I met with the student-coaches who had been together for the week-long class. Each shared stories of people they knew or had heard about that had experienced trauma. And each tale resonated with me at a very visceral level. I moved outside to the parking lot and stood beside our rental car. I began to vomit. Yes, in front of dozens of volunteers, professional health workers, equine specialists, and several guests, I puked my guts out.

Off to the side, I noticed a scramble of people. The stable owner and several volunteers were rushing around, talking on cellphones and, generally, behaving hurriedly and frantically. I heard the phrase "call the vet" several times. I hoped they weren't referring to me!

No. A horse we had arranged to be a part of the demonstrations was choking in the stall. "Yukon," the faithful and gentle leader of the Heavenly Acres herd, was in distress. There was widespread concern that, if not treated promptly, he would die. It was serious. Earlier that day, I had spent time with Yukon, assessing his suitability for EAL and, in specific, the exercises and demonstrations we had scheduled. To my experienced eye, he was outstanding and would make an excellent partner for the planned activity.

While the chaplain from the Armed Forces spent time with me and allowed me to voice my thoughts and feelings, an on-call veterinarian arrived to diagnose and assist the horse. There was nothing physically wrong with that incredible animal, but he had taken on my symptoms. Although he had never choked before or after and was one of the herd's healthiest horses, he was the one most deeply affected.

Within an hour of my "trigger" near the rental car in the parking lot, carloads of police officers, firefighters, soldiers, and spouses—all relieved of their duties due to the deep-seated effects of PTSD—arrived. As they exited their vehicles, I could see the sorrow and hopelessness in their faces

I had the opportunity to visit privately with each attendee. Their stories tore my heart. Witnessing death, notifying next of kin after a horrific accident, dealing with violence—the range of issues were numerous and deeply rooted. It was going to be a challenge.

A firefighter, who was now on long-term disability and whose life had turned upside down in a single evening, shared his story with me.

He was sitting alone on a low bench near the side of the arena, head in his hands and quietly weeping. As he related his experience, my heart broke. The man had been part of a crew fighting a structural fire. His platoon commander ordered the team to pull back from the building because of the danger to the firefighters and nearby structures.

The men withdrew, knowing there was a small child left inside. The child died. He could never forget the child's cries or the moral injury he has carried since that day nine years earlier.

I spoke with each of the men and women who had come to the demonstrations hoping and praying that, somehow, something would spark change in their lives. The female officer, ambushed, beaten, and raped while investigating a disturbance at a bar. There was the detective who had spent twenty years as the lead investigator on a homicide squad whose memories of a dismembered body haunt him every single night. And the Highway Patrol officer who had responded to six fatal accidents in only one week and had to notify the families of the deaths of their loved ones.

The stories were tragic, horrific, and terrifying. And the hearts, souls, and minds of these men and women were affected for a lifetime.

As part of the presentation and demonstration, I had designed an exercise that would illustrate the downward spiral of life that characterized people living with PTSD. It would involve the first responders present, and the critical figure would be one of the volunteers. In addition to my wife (who always works with me in EAL sessions), I had two other assistants. One was the chaplain, and the second was the owner of the farm. We substituted the ill "Yukon" for a mature horse named "Eddy." He would be the one to walk with the volunteer through the exercise.

Those in attendance formed a large circle around the perimeter of the arena. Those individuals symbolized characters in the victim's "normal" life: teachers, clerks, friends, fellow officers, their child's hockey coach, and everyday people they regularly met.

A second circle, inside the first, was marked with pylons. A third circle, still closer to the center, had also been drawn, and then a fourth at the very center. Each process represented the shrinking community of support that was available to those in agony over their injury.

The volunteer and horse walked around the outer circle, getting to know the personalities, life roles, and interactions in typical society. Then "the incident" happened. No longer was the officer enthused about going to a sporting event, meeting their child's teacher, or chatting with the clerk at the hardware store. And so, those representing the occupation and interactions that were no longer important left the circle. The individuals with whom the victim still wanted to remain in contact moved to the next ring closer to the center. They were the squadmates, family members, golf buddies, a best friend, and, of course, the horse, which represented their own heart.

But as the demonstration so vividly demonstrated, this circle of friends, family, buddies, and fellow officers would also change. Friends became weary of never being able to have a fun night with their pal. Squadmates returned to work and gradually stopped coming over to visit to see how the victim was doing. And the circle became smaller as those people left and went to stand along the side of the arena.

Now the circle of support shrank even more. Remaining were only the family members, the best friend, and the horse. This ring illustrated the deepening isolation that, almost universally, is felt by people with PTSD: the withdrawal, excessive sleep or no sleep, seclusion, and silent suffering. But their hearts—represented by the horse at their side—were still beating.

But the circle continued to contract. The family itself began to separate from the victim. The spouse needed social contact with others, even if the sufferer was unwilling to participate in that social contact. The children needed to get back to their sports, visit with friends, and share childhood joys. And the best friend, not knowing what to do, gradually became worn out, attempting to stay loyal to someone who just didn't care anymore.

The spiral continued until reaching the center. And all that remained were the volunteer representing the life of the person living with PTSD, and the horse, signifying the victim's heart. Still alive, still beating, but filled with sorrow, regret, anger, and numbness.

I watched as understanding flooded through the arena. From psychologists to teachers, the spectators in attendance, social workers, and spouses began to glimpse the dark and shadowed world lived by those with PTSD.

Understanding flooded the volunteer's mind and heart. Another helper entered and led her to the side to allow her to speak and process what had occurred. The arena was silent. Many wept.

Throughout my life as a cop, I had been witness to, or a participant in, events and circumstances that were truly horrible. However, I felt that it was "just part of the job" and never thought that my after-action was anything but ordinary. I denied that I had any form of PTSD. I wouldn't admit it, and I wouldn't seek help.

But now, with startling clarity, I began to admit that I, too, had PTSD. Those nightmares, cold sweats, mood swings, high anxiety, and health challenges were all symptoms of my occupational stress injury. What had begun that day to show others the symptomology of PTSD was, ultimately, a revelation for me. I began to recognize my warning signs and started my healing journey.

## CHAPTER THIRTY-TWO

It was a long flight back to our horse ranch. We had thoroughly enjoyed our time in Ontario, and the workshop on horses and trauma had been exceptionally well received by the students and organizers. However, the final day—doing the presentation and demonstration on PTSD—had impacted me more than I anticipated.

Once I understood that the feelings and actions I took in response to *my* traumatic incidents and circumstance were the root causes of some of the crazy stuff I did, I needed to know just what was happening.

I am not a doctor, psychologist, or social worker. I don't have the training or expertise to diagnose, treat, or comprehend the complex world of mental health issues. But I did serve for three decades as a cop, and the effects of that service—good and bad—linger.

So, what is post-traumatic stress injury? And what is the difference between PTSD and occupational stress injury (OSI)? As I talked with my doctor and a psychologist, I began to comprehend a bit more, to understand that there *is* a difference between the two, though they may be subtle and often interchanged.

Post-traumatic stress disorder is a mental condition that happens after a person experiences a traumatic event or feels a threat to their life. It triggers an increase in the flight/fight response. Like my experience, it can initiate damaging thoughts, feelings, and self-destructive actions. So, PTSD was both understandable and applicable. But what of OSI? How was it different?

Occupational stress injury is a non-medical term that suggests psychological difficulties after being in long-term, high-stress situations. Occupational stress injury does not happen due to a single event or experience but rather through constant exposure to traumatic incidents or experiences.

I believe the two terms, while similar and often interchanged, *are* fundamentally different. At its core, PTSD can happen after a single incident; OSI, however, is the result of long-term exposure to stressful events and takes time to develop and display its effects.

And their acceptance in the police community is also quite different. Many officers resist the PTSD label. They don't have difficulty with the words "post-traumatic stress" but are often troubled by the term "disorder." The implication is that the member is permanently messed up, with little or no hope of living a "normal" life. Also troubling is that many official forms, such as confidentiality agreements, gun registries, and security assignments, ask whether you have *ever had a mental disorder.* That can generate significant resistance to admitting you are struggling with stuff from the past.

However, the label of "occupational stress injury" is often far more accurate in describing an officer's symptoms after prolonged exposure to a stressful career and the hundreds of traumatic incidents to which he or she is exposed. And the word "injury" implies a possibility of healing or learning to cope, whereas "disorder" suggests a permanent condition.

But there is a third term that is coming into use that may be even more accurate in some circumstances—and that is *moral injury (MI)*.

Like the firefighter ordered to pull back from the burning apartment building while knowing there was a child left inside, some officers face dilemmas whose outcomes leave scars that last a lifetime. Unfair laws may be created by governments or applied to certain racial or ethnic groups (residential schools, Japanese internment camps, and the like). Or they may be subtler, such as the forced withdrawal of a criminal charge due to the perpetrator's wealth, political power, or standing in the community.

While PTSD focuses on symptoms associated with fear and OSI relates to long-term accumulated stressors, MI stems from being compelled to do something that is just not right, the decision made by someone with power and authority over the officer. Not often spoken about, MI is real and more common than admitted.

None of the diagnoses—PTSD, OSI, or MI—are in any way indicative of a flawed character, lack of willpower, or weakness. The three designations begin externally but end internally. They do not define us, nor do they have to limit our ability to live and enjoy a happy and fulfilling life.

Yes, those moments will come when a sight, sound, smell, touch, or even a taste trigger a memory, and the emotions flood back. I recognize that these will come when I least expect them, and often at the most inopportune times.

Social media is full of memes, trite sayings, and shared posts that attempt to address the broad issues of PTSD, OSI, and MI. You can even buy posters with proverbs in bright colors that advise *Let's Just Talk*, or *It's Not What Happens to You, It's What You Do about What Happens to You,* and *Look on the Bright Side.* But the big question is this: WHO can you talk with that can empathize? What *can* you do about what happened to you? *What* bright side?

Those who have patrolled the streets of hell can't explain, and those who have not patrolled the streets of hell can't understand.

Why is the subject of PTSD so tricky to both talk about and understand? It is, in part, the nature of the incident or incidents themselves. They don't lend themselves to casual conversations. How do you talk to someone about mangled bodies, horrific murders, or terrifying confrontations? How do you tell a parent their child has died?

The responses can be similar—*oh, that must have been horrible, I can't imagine doing that myself,* or, *if it's so bad, why don't you just quit?*

Expressions of sympathy and encouraging support are sincerely yet naïvely offered—*you're so tough and brave, you'll make it*, or, sometimes even more troubling, *just talk it out, you'll feel better.*

And it's difficult at times to talk to superiors or department psychologists. There's a stigma attached to being seen as weak, a scofflaw, or neglecting your duty. *Leave the job at work and don't take it home* was a typical response from superiors. But just how do you leave your thoughts, sorrows, and experiences behind when the uniform comes off? You can't.

And PTSD, OSI, and MI are on the rise. The increased call-load and severity of those calls and the increased restrictions and political correctness permeate all of society. Where once patrol units would gather mid-shift at a coffee shop to chat and debrief about the last call they were on, that is now frowned upon or, in many cases, forbidden. Getting together wasn't a time to enjoy the coffee and donuts. Still, it was an opportunity to meet with peers who understood your anxiety or pain, a chance for you to share it with folks who could understand.

Black humor was prevalent and a way of coping with horrific scenes and their devastation on the attending officers. But now, with cellphones capturing every moment, a sharp crack made at the scene of a fatal accident had the high probability of landing the officer in Internal Affairs. So, the officer bottles the emotion up inside.

But there is change happening. Small groups are getting together in support of each other. Whether on private social media groups or at ten a.m. at a local café, ways are being found. And there is a rising awareness of the devastation caused by PTSD on individuals, families, and the community itself. Resources and training to recognize and assist the people with PTSD and OSI are being initiated. Most encouraging is the recognition of the need for peer-to-peer support.

And veterans are now speaking out. Not bound by political correctness or departmental policy or oversight, they speak unfiltered and unrestrained. They speak from the heart.

## CHAPTER THIRTY-THREE

After the murder of my partner, I became a drunk. That was my way of dealing with nightmares, sorrow, and guilt. Did it work? Yes, for short periods, it did. But only to get me through the night. Then the feelings were back again in the morning. I engaged in hazardous stunts. Why? Maybe because I needed to feel fully alive. Perhaps it was a socially acceptable alternative to withdrawal and depression. "Death by Moose" would have been a far more exciting headline than "Officer Commits Suicide."

Over the years, I learned that I could not chase the nightmares. I had to wall them off and stop them from filling my brain during those shadowy midnights. My wife bought me a special blanket whose weight covering gives me an almost womb-like comfort, and I still use it on occasion. I learned not to drink coffee after mid-day. I limited my alcohol. As one old sergeant said, "Ross, it's not *what* you drink or even how *much* you drink; it's *WHY* you drink that's the concern."

Dee understood the chaos of my life—from quitting the RCMP, to jumping from job to job, to getting back into policing. She did not judge, nag, or harass—just listened, supported, and gently guided me back to calmness when I would become overwhelmed. And times when nightmares crept through the barriers and my body shook with fear, she put her hand on my chest and calmed my terror. My "midnight angel."

It wasn't just the killing of my partner that panicked my mind, but the numerous calls and experiences I'd accumulated. Each one separate and distinct yet blending into one another as time compressed them and pushed healthy thoughts to the side.

It was a long time before I began to understand that dealing with death is a process. And coming to grips with the murder of a friend and colleague took time. It started with disbelief and shock. *That can't be true! That can't happen!* Then it morphed into anger at the senselessness and pointlessness of his death. It wasn't during a robbery or shoot-out. It was cold-blooded, and he didn't have a chance to fight back. I then tried to justify why I was still alive. Why had Donny taken the call and not me? There was no reasoning, so my risky actions took on close-to-death activities. Later, I pulled into a shell and wouldn't discuss or even talk about it.

Depression? I don't know, that's for people more educated than I to figure out, but I knew I had moments of sadness, regret, and sorrow.

But, as time passed and I learned more and more to trust that God was in control (although I did blame Him from time to time), I began to accept that my partner gave his life in a great cause—maintaining rightness in a wrongness world.

While many incidents impacted my life as a front-line police officer, the drowning of the babies that cold, rainy night haunts my soul to this day. It's an occurrence that, while of short duration, had life-long consequences for those involved.

What did I learn, and how did I cope with the murder of four small children—two of them babies? I have struggled with that for many years. I still cannot comprehend the mother's horrific act of throwing her little girls off the bridge and into the freezing water.

There were, and are, many speculations and theories as to why she did what she did, but she *did* do it. But I was there to carry the babies home to their Heavenly Father, and, for that, I felt privileged. It could have been anyone, but it was me who happened to be there.

I genuinely believe that God put me in that spot at that time to carry the babies home to Him. He gave me that honor.

While the murder of my partner and the drowning of the children had significant impacts on my life, they were single occurrences that occurred in truly short timeframes. From a clinical standpoint, they were clear examples of incidents that created PTSD conditions, isolated events with long-term effects.

My time as the Vice-Unit commander was different. I had the authority and resources to restructure the unit and improve its administrative efficiency and operational effectiveness. In short, I went into it knowing I could do something positive. While I wasn't sure what that "something" was, I was confident that changes were possible.

During my time in Vice, I attended thirteen funerals—all girls under eighteen. And all had lost their lives on the streets. AIDS, drug overdoses, suicides, and homicides.

As part of our one-day presentations to teachers, parents, and social service providers, I wrote a short true-story account of one girls' journey from her first contact with a pimp through to her tragic death. I read it to the participants, and the 2,000-word *High Heels and Teddy Bears* article began to circulate through the community.

Attendees at these presentations asked me to provide other true stories of these kids' heartbreaking lives, and as I completed and shared each account, the demand increased.

A contact in New York invited me to speak to the United Nations' unique mission. The Special Rapporteur held a series of "discovery" meetings on the worldwide phenomena of children's sale and sexual exploitation. Their mandate was to identify emerging patterns, coordinate best prevention practices, and identify rehabilitation measures. Upon the conclusion of my presentation, I shared several of the articles I had written with the committee.

With encouragement from those attending the Special Rapporteur session, I began to expand the stories into a more extensive work, which eventually formed the book, *Children in The Game*.

Writing the book and viewing the subsequent film based on the stories (*The Butterfly Collectors*) was one method of keeping the children's memories alive.

Working in the Vice area of policing was tough. Lobbying for new legislation or attempting to amend existing laws was frustrating. Resources were scarce, the public uninformed, and most political leaders apathetic. But we kept trying and gratefully saw small but incremental changes take place. Through the wisdom and insights of the Knights of the Round Table, I was able to organize and execute a strategic plan that, over several years, began to produce positive results.

My family also became involved in this effort. My wife would accompany me at night as I responded to the calls from the kids. My son and daughter would drive the van as we checked on, and visited with, those youngsters who had no home, no family, and, often, no hope.

The work on the streets—with kids viciously exploited, some losing their lives, and "the system" seemly unable to give the issue the priority it needed—took its toll. Its effect on me was different from that of short-term traumatic incidents. It was pervasive and long term.

But I also learned that if I focussed on the mission and not on the administrative requirements, I could continue. If I gathered around me people who shared that purpose, I could remain effective and dedicated.

# CHAPTER THIRTY-FOUR

Towards the end of my policing career, I had the opportunity to attend a by-invitation-only course at the Canadian Police College, the senior police administrator course (SPAC). The curriculum drew students from around the world. High-ranking members from such diverse police organizations as Bermuda, Hong Kong, and Surinam forces, the FBI, and the New South Wales State Police in Australia joined Canadian delegates for an intense six weeks of discussion, policy review, and analysis of past activities and future visions.

It was one of the most intense and valuable programs I attended over my decades of policing. And while the lectures and round-table discussions were robust and insightful, the informal sessions held in the barracks were the most revealing. The combined years of service within this group exceeded 800 on the street, and their insights into law and order were without parallel at any other place and time.

While many informal discussions turned around matters such as bail reform, prosecutorial discretion, and rehabilitation restructurings, social-justice issues produced the most emotion.

The opportunity to visit with officers from around the world was given to very few. Delegates related incidents of apartheid in South Africa, ghettoization in the U.S., eminent-domain seizures in the United Kingdom, and class privilege in the Caribbean. There was a significant number of senior police from the various Canadian agencies, and more than a few raised the Indian Act's taboo subject.

During those unofficial discussions, police officers (almost all with more than twenty years of service) freely expressed feelings of regret, frustration, and even sorrow. Several of the members present had also been a part of the forced removal of children from the First Nations reserves under the federal government's mandate. At this late stage in their careers, they still felt helpless to address the injustice meted out or make sense of a policy they did not enact but did enforce.

I was not alone.

And while the instructors raised the subjects of PTSD and OSI and recommended steps for mitigation and recovery, there did not seem to be a path forward in dealing with MI issues. Attending officers discussed it, and members were transparent and forthcoming about their own experiences, yet there did not seem to be any priority given to its resolution or healing. Each member was left to wrestle with the issue as best they could. It was an unsatisfactory conclusion.

I had never discussed the subject with anyone before. Quite frankly, I had not even raised the matter with my family until years after my retirement. I was at a total loss on ways to deal with those memories.

In its early years, the RCMP was the government's sole representative for dealing with Aboriginal issues. However, it wasn't long before those in political power appointed bureaucrats (Indian agents) to administer social programs and control treaty benefits. The RCMP relegated to the role of enforcer of the Indian Act, including the authority to force attendance at the residential schools and return "truant" students to the institutions.

Organizational change sometimes happens from inside and sometimes from outside pressures. In the dealings with Aboriginal issues, it was a bit of both. At about the time of my service, the force recognized that their long and sometimes challenging role with Indigenous communities in Canada needed to transform. The RCMP made many policies and procedure changes through hiring practices and special constables' appointments of Aboriginal or Metis descent.

Attendance and presentations by members at various First Nations schools began to rebuild the force's relationship with the local Indigenous populations. Later, senior RCMP managers would form special directorates to coordinate and more effectively deliver policing services to reserves.

In 1994, Commissioner Giuliano Zaccardelli publicly apologized for the RCMP's role in the Residential School System. Then again, in 2014, Commissioner Bob Paulson apologized as part of the Truth and Reconciliation Commission's national event.

And the force took a crucial role in such actions as the Missing and Murdered Aboriginal Women. They also established the Aboriginal Community Constable program, transferred cemetery land back to Aboriginal control, and added First Nations content to Depot's training curriculum. These and other similar efforts slowly began healing the rift of the previous 150 years.

While the various commissioners' efforts and those of the organization itself were laudable, their long-term effectiveness is still to be determined.

But missing from these commendable efforts was a key component—the effect that the Indian Act's enforcement had on *individual* members of the RCMP themselves.

The informal chats with the senior officers at the Canadian Police College were comforting, in some ways, for revealing I was not alone in my regrets. Several of them had also been in detachments that required them to enforce the Indian Act and the residential school system. But while there may be some truth in the phrase "misery loves company," we understood that each of us would have to wrestle the demons of our mind on our own.

★ ★ ★

First Nations peoples of Western Canada have a long and reverent relationship with horses that dates back hundreds of years. Yet, in modern times, with the advent of motorized vehicles, social media, and culture loss, many band members have lost the skills relating to equines.

I had grown up in an era and community where horses were a mainstay—used for work, pleasure, and companionship. Later, my formal training in horsemanship with the RCMP enabled me to increase my skills and understanding of these amazing animals. Maybe, just maybe, this was an opportunity for me to connect with and walk alongside Aboriginal men as they recaptured a portion of their heritage. And perhaps I could also learn some of the "old ways" from them.

By working with First Nations' communities as they began training their group of "wildies," I started to get a greater sense of the lost culture and the desire to regain that contact and heritage.

Over the next few years, it was my honor to lead EAL groups at several Aboriginal communities in Western Canada. And at each one, I learned more than I taught. I became more aware of how significant horses are to this population's culture. I did not have a single student who did not love gaining a deeper understanding of the horse and the skills required to gentle and ride these animals, which were such a rich part of their heritage.

But there was a sadness present as well. I got to know and became close friends with many of the students, elders, and council members. I began to learn more about the loss of culture over the generations. All the students knew a parent, grandparent, or great-grandparent who was forcibly removed to a residential school. Over the intervening generations, the skills and horse knowledge, once fundamental to culture and survival, gradually became lost. But the memories were kept alive through the relating of stories, songs, and dances.

Although I now spent considerable time with the Indigenous communities, I did not share my past association with the residential schools or the Sixties Scoop. Frankly, I didn't dare. I was afraid that the friendships gained would be lost if they knew about it. But I did feel that I would sense the time and place was right at some point, and it would be then that I would bare my soul—and accept whatever outcome arose.

And it did. It was mid-summer, and we received a call from a Cree First Nations community in north-central Alberta. They had learned of our program and work using horses for trauma healing. They asked if we would be open to conducting a five-day program in their community and begin teaching the methodology of using horses as a partner in coaching individuals toward self-healing and the development of sustainable programs within the community. It was an honor to accept the invitation.

# CHAPTER THIRTY-FIVE

We arrived in the Cree community on a Sunday evening and, orienting ourselves, prepared our material for the coming week. Due to the group's anticipated size, we had asked for assistance from several other coaches with EAL Canada. One was a psychologist with long experience in counseling, one was a coach who had done a lot of work with First Nations communities in British Columbia, and we brought a wrangler from our ranch to help with the horses. Backstopping the cadre of instructors was a Metis woman from northern Alberta who had operated a similar program in her community for several years.

The first morning we were greeted by the largest group we had ever taught. Greeting us on that Monday morning was a total of twenty-two students. The group included the director of health services, a band council member, an elder, and five riders of the Indian Horse Relay Team, which had just competed in a regional rodeo. It was a diverse group, with some having extensive knowledge of horses and horsemanship, some with backgrounds in addiction counseling, and a few who had limited exposure to either. It promised to be a thought-provoking week.

The day began with the traditional exchange of gifts. The elder then stood and spoke a prayer in the Cree language, followed by a "smudge" with sweetgrass. This ceremony was to be followed each day of the course and became one of the high points each morning. It allowed the day to begin in a spirit of reverence, calmness, and thankfulness.

As part of our research and from the director of Health Services' knowledge, we focused our theory on trauma issues. Direct trauma, indirect trauma, trans-generational trauma, and compassion exhaustion. Each segment pertained to individuals in the group as well as to the community. We also talked about the residential school program's long-term effects and the Sixties Scoop – an area where I struggled. I was teaching healing when I, myself, needed to heal.

But the days continued. Each afternoon was "horse time," and exercises were designed to allow each student to fill both coach and client roles. Several members of the community brought in horses. Some were well-broke and rideable—others, not so much. But the students used every horse in the various exercises and demonstrations.

One of the horses brought to the arena was eye-catching and incredibly majestic. Predominately black with white markings, seven years old, and recently gelded, the magnificent animal stood out from the rest. Just over sixteen hands in height, the horse was a gorgeous animal with a regal bearing. The mustang had a gentle eye but an attitude of "Are you good enough to be around me?" I was intrigued. He was owned, led, and handled by the elder, Percy Moosepayo.

As is my practice, I checked each horse for health and temperament before working with students or clients. Rubbing the spine to get any indication of soreness, checking the head, neck, and body for flexibility and injuries, and lifting each foot to check for soundness and "give." Percy's horse was the last one in the line for me to examine.

I approached and held out my hand in greeting. The horse sniffed, then softly blew on the back of my fingers. It was going to be an easy check, I thought. I gently examined neck and poll, then ran my hand down the animal's sides and back. Healthy and strong. No injuries or any sign of soreness. I went to pick up his feet.

With speed five times faster than a professional boxer, the horse lifted his hind leg, kicked out, caught me on the inside of my thigh, and tossed me like a rag doll halfway across the arena! I rose unsteadily to my feet and limped back to Percy and the big horse. Percy just grinned. "He hasn't had much handling," he said. I looked at the horse, and I do believe he was smiling, as well.

Out of that incident, which took me down a peg or two, Percy and I quickly became friends. I felt a deep connection with the horse and had the sense he would teach me a lot.

The following day, Percy brought the horse to the middle of the arena and motioned me over. There was a brief "recess" in the program, so we were alone.

He asked me to stand on the left side, nearest the horse's heart. Percy stood on the right. He had me place my hands on the horse's spine.

"I sense that you need to talk," he said, as he placed his hands atop of mine. How he knew what was on my heart, I will never know. But he discerned a hurt in me and invited me to share.

We stood in that position for a half-hour, the horse never moving. I poured out the guilt, sorrow, and sadness that I had carried all these years. I talked of my role in the apprehension of children from reserves. I shared my memory of my part in the residential school injustices and the scoop of children taken by Social Services as I stood by and did nothing. I told him of my shame that I did not step forward and challenge this injustice, but instead took the easier way and quit the RCMP entirely. He pressed my hands closer to the horse.

I did not apologize—it seemed so hollow to do so. I did not justify or try to mitigate my involvement, nor did I blame the force or even the government. It was my struggle, and I had to own it.

There was silence as I finished my story. We remained in that position for several moments as the elder meditated on it.

"I will think about this," he said, at last. "Just stay with the horse awhile and let him speak to you."

With that, he lifted his hands from mine, stepped back, and moved away. As Percy withdrew from the horse, a truly magical moment occurred. The horse breathed a huge sigh, lowered his head, and shifted his weight against me. To have a 1,200-pound, sentient presence leaning on me and giving his breath and heartbeat to me was a wonderful, powerful lesson. He had accepted me.

Several minutes passed as I stood with the horse. It was a calming and supportive time with the tall animal leaning against me and my body bearing the weight shifted to me. I gradually stepped away. The horse resumed a normal stance, then turned and looked at me. As I slowly walked toward the wall of the arena, he followed.

Percy was waiting at the end of the sand-covered floor, and I walked to him. I had draped the lead rope over the horse's neck. I now lifted it and handed the end to the elder. He took it and turned to leave the building.

"We'll talk tomorrow," he said as he led the horse out the door. I felt strangely alone yet at peace as the pair disappeared.

It was with mixed feelings that I entered the arena the following day. During the morning, I worked with the students on several subjects relating to the horse's power to heal from trauma. Just before lunch, we concluded the exercises. A leader gathered the students and a few other band members in a circle near the corrals.

I did not participate in the talking circle, electing to sit outside the group and listen as they shared their stories. The process began with a prayer and a sweetgrass smudge. As the leader moved around the group, each person stood. The smoke from the sweetgrass rose from the sacred stone on which it lay smoldering, and, using a feather, the leader fanned it upward. Each participant, in turn, using their open hands, drew the smoke toward them. Gently waving the wisps to their heart and head, they "washed" themselves in the aromatic smoke.

The leader then passed the feather to the first member of the group and invited him to speak. Only one person voiced their story as the others remained silent and listened. The speaker then passed the feather to the next, and each member expressed what lay heaviest on their heart.

I sat listening as person after person shared their thoughts of violence in the community. They told of a family member's drug addiction, the hopelessness of poverty, the sorrow of suicides, and their fear for their children and grandchildren. Many expressed their sadness for the loss of culture through the residential school system. Others were victims of being taken from their families and placed in foster care with no knowledge of their history or family lineage.

It was the first time I had heard the personal stories of the wounds created through a policy that dated back to previous centuries and that only recently began to be addressed. I knew that I had been a part of that sorrow.

# CHAPTER THIRTY-SIX

"Did you learn?" Percy asked as we stood together later that afternoon. He did not ask, "Did you hear?" He asked if I had learned.

I nodded. "Yes, I did learn."

"I have spoken to the other elders," he said quietly. "And they felt honored that you have spoken and shared your troubles." He put his hand on my shoulder as we made our way back to the group. "And it is enough that you have learned."

Although I had not sought understanding or acceptance, it had been given.

Throughout the week, we did many exercises and demonstrations with the horses from the community. Some had previous training, and some did not, and one or two were close to being feral. For some, this was their first time inside a building. It had been an incredible five days of teaching and learning, but it was ending.

We conducted the final assignment on the morning of the last day. The exercise, designed by the students, involved two horses and six members of the community. The working name given to the task was "The Wounded Warrior," founded on the tradition that no warrior is left behind on the field of battle.

A single "warrior" stood in place across the arena, representing an individual who was wounded and in need of assistance. The wounds described were not from a battle with guns, arrows, clubs, or knives. The injuries presented were from loneliness, addiction, betrayal, and hopelessness. The five remaining members took positions directly across from the warrior, about a hundred feet away. The students placed two empty chairs within the group and piled a neat stack of robes and blankets.

The warrior slid down to a sitting position, conveying the message of dejection and sorrow. He raised his hand and signaled the five that he needed help. Two members of the group, each leading a horse, walked forward to the seated man. Then, each "rescuer" acted together, took an arm of the one needing help, and lifted him to his feet.

Gently and with great compassion, and with the horses close beside, they walked with the wounded warrior across the sand to the remaining group and the two chairs. A grandmother sat in one of the chairs, and the robes and blankets now rested on her lap.

The two rescuers presented the wounded man to the woman, who invited him to sit beside her. He did so. As he settled in the chair, the remaining members unfolded the robes and blankets and wrapped them around him and the older woman seated alongside him.

The woman took the hands of the man and held them to her heart. She spoke words in the Cree language that I did not understand, but the words spoken brought tears to his eyes, and he sobbed. She did not heal him, but the warrior was rescued and taken to a healing place.

My wife and I had been teaching EAL for almost twenty years but had never witnessed a demonstration so powerful and meaningful.

I did not ask *who* the wounded warrior represented, but I had the profound sense that the elder had influenced the demonstration just for me. It was as if the Creator had brought me, a wounded man, to this place of healing. My sorrow and guilt over the injustice of the past were now beginning to heal. A sense of reconciliation settled on my soul.

It was an emotional day, as the students, family members, and instructors gathered to enjoy and celebrate the course's close and engage in the traditional exchange of gifts.

The director of Health Services presented Dee with a delicately beaded likeness of a grizzly-bear paw. There were five claws. One claw represented the "singleness" of all creation, and the four separate ones depicted the four directions, four seasons, and four elements. The central pad was in the form of a heart, and the entire paw was mounted on black leather and surrounded by silver conchos. Dee presented the director with a gift from EAL Canada to assist in developing their equine youth program.

Then the elder came forward. He presented to me a knot of colored ribbons. The ribbons represented horses and, as protection for the herd, were to be hung in our home, truck, or stable. I accepted them with honor and appreciation. But there was more.

From his breast pocket, he produced a turquoise amulet in the shape of a horse created by a Navajo friend. I would wear it on a light chain around my neck to protect my body and heart from injury and hurt. The gifts given to me were emotional and meaningful. But there was still more.

The elder who had allowed me to share my past now brought a small aspen branch in full leaf. He presented it to me. I had no idea what this represented or the meaning behind such a gift.

"You know that horse that you love so much?" he asked. "He is now yours."

I was stunned. Percy had given me his best horse. Tradition and culture recognize that this is one of the most important and meaningful gifts an elder can bestow—the gift of *his* horse.

I stood before him; the Aspen branch clutched in my hands and tears of gratitude and humility running down my cheeks. It was an incredible honor. I could not speak words that would, in any understandable way, express my feelings or emotions. I stumbled with a response that must have sounded almost incomprehensible. I honored his gift and the meaning behind it. I voiced my deep gratitude, then asked, "What is his name?"

He looked at me and replied, "He has no name." If I stumbled with words before, now I was speechless. I recalled an old song about traveling through a desert on a horse with no name.

The elder continued. "I have watched you and listened to you through this past week, and I feel you need the horse, and the horse needs you. I will think upon this, and when you return, I will give the name to your horse."

We completed our work in the community and returned home without the horse. We had not taken a trailer with us, so we would return later to bring "No-Name" back to our ranch.

During the intervening months, I prepared to receive him. We built a new corral to accommodate No-Name, allowing the horse to transition safely to the new herd. It would let the other horses approach, sniff, challenge, or accept as they desired. But the wooden rails surrounding the corral would prevent fights or injury. By late summer, it was ready.

I also learned that the song containing the words, "I've been through the desert on a horse with no name," performed by the group America, was written by Dewey Bunnell. He related that the phrase was a metaphor for getting away from life's confusion and pain and entering a quiet, peaceful place. Wow.

As planned, we returned to the Cree First Nation Community. Overnighting in a nearby town, we arrived at the elder's home the next morning. Dee and I met Percy and his wife, and we moved to the corral.

The horse was standing in all his magnificence, looking directly at me. He seemed to know we were soon to be together. The elder slipped a halter over the horse-with-no-name and brought him from the corral. He handed the lead rope to me.

"I prayed and thought for many hours on his name, and I have received it." He paused. "He is to be called NiChi. In our language, NiChi means 'friend.' One who is closer than a brother. One who travels together." The elder repeated. "He is to be called NiChi."

I walked with NiChi across the lawn and down the laneway. He moved fluidly and willingly by my side. When I stopped, he stood quietly beside me for a moment, then, arching his neck, took my old cowboy hat in his teeth, removed it from my head, and stood there holding it. I chuckled. It was going to be a partnership I would treasure. He knew it, too.

My heart was at peace.

## CHAPTER THIRTY-SEVEN

Someone once said that life is a series of peaks and valleys, and, to go to the mountain, one must go through the valley. And all of us, including you, the reader, have been through many valleys.

As mortals, we focus our thoughts and feelings on those valleys we have come through, as dark and traumatic as they may have been. And we retain them in our minds and hearts for a lifetime, never seeming to have the strength to move outward and onward and to climb those paths that lead to a more fulfilling life.

Or we reject the very memories of those times and push the darkness to the far reaches of our soul, determined never to let their recollection enter our conversations, confessions, or thoughts. And, although they may sneak through in the darkness of night, we do our absolute best to deny their existence.

But I believe life is like two parallel paths, leading from the past to the future. One course denotes struggle and, oft-times, sorrow, and regret. The other is optimism, challenge, and achievement. We get to choose on which path to focus.

And in choosing the path forward, we realize life itself is a do-it-yourself kind of project. We are in charge.

But we cannot heal alone.

We cannot rewrite our histories. We cannot wipe out the fact that we have seen horrific things and witnessed events that are just plain wrong.

The way to return to a path of hope is to reprocess the way we have judged ourselves, others, and the world that has allowed atrocities to occur.

When we face fear, shame, and discouragement, we want to isolate ourselves. But we need the support and love of our family and friends to restore our world.

We need to gain wisdom from our experiences. And we are called to find new meaning in our lives that can energize and direct us to a more purposeful one.

We have a choice.

We can become victims of our traumas and the automatic thoughts that come from them, *or* we can realize we went through all this for some purpose and now must do the work to push through to new vistas of growth.

Gaining wisdom from our experiences does not imply that we minimize the incidents that created the conditions for trauma or suggest that we have forgotten them. In moving forward and creating a life worth living, we have learned to manage those stressors.

It took many years and the support of a whole team for me to come to an understanding that, while I could not change the circumstances of the past, I could learn from them and become someone better. I learned acceptance, compassion, forgiveness, and reconciliation—tough lessons.

After the murder of my partner, I went through a period of alcohol abuse, recriminations, and questioning why he was killed and not me. I embarked on an almost suicidal drive for risk. But over time, I understood that I could control the trauma's effects on me, even while I could not control the incident. It may have defined the character of Charles Hill, who pulled the trigger and killed Donny, but it did not need to define me or my life after the event.

The drowning of the babies was, without question, the most impactful and personal experience of my life. To witness evil and be helpless to prevent its destructive power was devastating. Without the friendship of an old gang of streetwise people I met for breakfast, I do not think I would have come through it. Ultimately, their wisdom and compassion and the words spoken to me by a retired madam allowed my heart to find a level of peace. Her words didn't mitigate the horror, but they permitted me space to see my role in the tragic events.

There was nothing I could have done to prevent these tragedies from occurring. And there was little positive action I could take in the aftermath. My experience in the Vice Unit, however, was different. There, I could reduce the occurrences of children's sexual enslavement—and I decided to do so. Lobbying for legal changes, speaking at conferences and the United Nations, going on talk shows, writing and distributing a book, and even commissioning a television short, were ways of fighting back. Taking some form of action was something I *could* do. And I did. It did not eliminate child prostitution, but it did lessen it. And it did raise awareness across the country and encourage other jurisdictions to take similar steps. Could I have done more? Possibly. But I did *something*.

The issues and generational trauma caused by the Indian Act's enforcement, residential schools, and the Sixties Scoop were quite different from criminals' acts. These were actions initiated by the government and enforced by front-line officers. And they had more far-reaching effects than any single deed of a criminal mind.

For years I blamed governments, senior officers, and social programs. I justified the actions with: "I was only following orders," "It was the laws of the time," and "I resigned because of it, so showed resistance."

But the reality was, I was a part of the problem and did nothing. I did not even speak of it until many years after my retirement, and then only to my family members and one close friend. Although I did workshops and clinics for First Nations communities through the years and conducted youth programs both on and off the reserves, I could not acknowledge my shame of being a part of that system.

When I met the elder, I told my story and revealed my past. He did not judge me, condemn me, or give me advice. He listened. He accepted. He respected my admission. And, as he had experienced the generational trauma as well, he understood.

And he honored me with the gifting of his horse.

And through that act, I can write about it now with full disclosure.

I had mentioned earlier that life itself is a kind of do-it-yourself project. And through my life, I discovered that incredible change happens when you decide to control over which you have power. And I have power over my thoughts and my mind. The transformation is not quick or inevitable but an ongoing effort. It's a daily workout for the mind, soul, and spirit.

I look around me today with deep gratitude. If I did not go through the experiences I did, I would not be the man I am today—healthy, loved, at peace. But still a work in progress.

I am so thankful for the blessings I have received. For over five decades, Dee and I have been together, and our children—Heather and Jordie—are in great marriages. I have six grandchildren and many friends. I have a ranch in the foothills of the Rocky Mountains, horses, and purpose in my life.

But I cannot eliminate PTSD or OSI from my heart and mind. They are not temporary conditions, nor are they things that have an end. They are thoughts, feelings, and memories to be managed each day and night.

What is my definition of success? It is this: Success is taking what you've learned from your parents, grandparents, mentors, and life itself, applying those lessons to your journey, and then passing them on to others.

I hope that I have done so.

# ACKNOWLEDGEMENTS

I had the help of many in the writing of this book. Firstly, was my wife Dee and our children, Heather and Jordie. Many of the details were previously unknown to them, but they encouraged me to tell my story and provided incredible support as the journey unfolded. I love them deeply.

The readers of the early drafts were central to ensuring the accuracy of details and the symptomology of PTSD, OSI, and Moral Injury. Individually and collectively, they made the book much better than initially written. A huge thanks to Dr. Karen Badenhorst, Bev Carter-Buffalo, Jack Busst, Amanda Moosepayo, Nancy Janssens, Adam Kaine, Dr. Gaye Kropf, Jody Reid Latta, Julie Letal, Percy Moosepayo, and Graham Tomalty

A heartfelt tribute to Chief Superintendent Lloyd Hickman (Retired) whose insights refined the details of RCMP training at Depot, and key points on policies and procedures. Sadly, Lloyd passed away before this book was published. He was a man deeply admired and respected. He was my friend. We will miss him.

Concerning the editing and publishing process, I wish to thank the wonderful folk at Friesen Press. Debbie Anderson and Julianne McCallum shepherded this book through the winding path of the publishing process. Your insights, encouragement, and yes, even timelines brought everything together to produce the completed work.

Jennifer Clifford inspired the cover image, and I treasure her talent and dedication. And the team of editors, designers, and resource folk at Friesen are the best in the business.

And especially to my readers. You are the reason I write. Thank you.

# CONTACT THE AUTHOR

Ross MacInnes is an experienced, knowledgeable, and entertaining speaker. He has presented keynotes, break-out sessions, and workshops throughout North America. To check out his other books, or to contact him directly, go to https://rossamacinnes.com/

CPSIA information can be obtained
at www.ICGtesting.com
Printed in the USA
BVHW030543140521
607207BV00003B/22